by John R. Levine
and
Margaret Levine Young

IDG Books Worldwide, Inc.
An International Data Group Company
San Mateo, California ♦ Indianapolis, Indiana ♦ Boston, Massachusetts

The Internet For Dummies Quick Reference

Published by
IDG Books Worldwide, Inc.
An International Data Group Company
155 Bovet Road, Suite 310
San Mateo, CA 94402

Library of Congress Catalog Card No.: 94-75909

ISBN: 1-56884-168-X

Printed in the United States of America

10 9 8 7 6 5 4 3 2

Distributed in the United States by IDG Books Worldwide, Inc.

Distributed in Canada by Macmillan of Canada, a Division of Canada Publishing Corporation; by Computer and Technical Books in Miami, Florida, for South America and the Caribbean; by Longman Singapore in Singapore, Malaysia, Thailand, and Korea; by Toppan Co. Ltd. in Japan; by Asia Computerworld in Hong Kong; by Woodslane Pty. Ltd. in Australia and New Zealand; and by Transword Publishers Ltd. in the U.K. and Europe.

For general information on IDG Books in the U.S., including information on discounts and premiums, contact IDG Books at 800-762-2974 or 415-312-0650.

For information on where to purchase IDG Books outside the U.S., contact Christina Turner at 415-312-0633.

For information on translations, contact Marc Jeffrey Mikulich, Foreign Rights Manager, at IDG Books Worldwide; FAX NUMBER 415-358-1260.

For sales inquiries and special prices for bulk quantities, write to the address above or call IDG Books Worldwide at 415-312-0650.

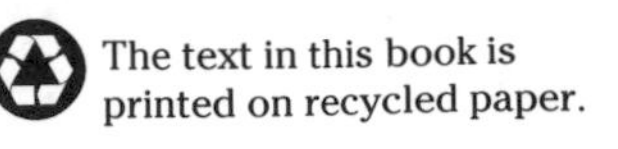

About the Authors

John Levine and **Margaret Levine Young** were members of a computer club in high school (this was before high school students — or even high schools — *had* computers). They came in contact with Theodor H. Nelson, the author of *Computer Lib* and the inventor of hypertext, who fostered the idea that computers should not be taken seriously. He showed them that everyone can understand and use computers. John would like to thank Ted for letting him hole up on his houseboat during the final editing for this book.

John wrote his first program in 1967 on an IBM 1130 (a computer roughly as powerful as your typical modern digital wristwatch — only more difficult to use). His first exposure to the Internet was while working part-time for Interactive Systems, the first commercial UNIX company, and his system was listed in the earliest map of Usenet (see Part 3 of this book) published in *Byte* in 1981. He used to spend most of his time writing software, but now he mostly writes books because it's more fun. He wrote *UNIX For Dummies* and *Unix For Dummies Quick Reference* with Margy and *The Internet For Dummies* with Carol Baroudi. He also teaches some computer courses and publishes and edits an incredibly technoid magazine called *The Journal of C Language Translation* for which all of the authors submit their articles by e-mail via the Internet. He has a B.A. and Ph.D. in computer science from Yale University.

Margy has been using small computers since the 1970s. She graduated from UNIX on a PDP/11 to Apple DOS on an Apple II to MS-DOS and UNIX on a variety of machines. She has done all kinds of jobs that involve explaining to people that computers aren't as mysterious as they might think, including managing the use of PCs at Columbia Pictures, teaching scientists and engineers what computers are good for, and writing computer manuals. She has been president of NYPC, the New York PC Users' Group. Margy has written several computer books, including *Understanding Javelin PLUS* (John also wrote part of it), *The Complete Guide to PC-File, UNIX For Dummies* (with John) and *WordPerfect For Windows For Dummies* (with David C. Kay). She has a degree in computer science from Yale University.

ABOUT IDG BOOKS WORLDWIDE

Welcome to the world of IDG Books Worldwide.

IDG Books Worldwide, Inc., is a subsidiary of International Data Group, the world's largest publisher of business and computer-related information and the leading global provider of information services on information technology. IDG was founded more than 25 years ago and now employs more than 5,700 people worldwide. IDG publishes more than 200 computer publications in 63 countries (see listing below). Forty million people read one or more IDG publications each month.

Launched in 1990, IDG Books is today the fastest-growing publisher of computer and business books in the United States. We are proud to have received 3 awards from the Computer Press Association in recognition of editorial excellence, and our best-selling ...*For Dummies* series has more than 10 million copies in print with translations in more than 20 languages. IDG Books, through a recent joint venture with IDG's Hi-Tech Beijing, became the first U.S. publisher to publish a computer book in the People's Republic of China. In record time, IDG Books has become the first choice for millions of readers around the world who want to learn how to better manage their businesses.

WINNER
Eighth Annual Computer Press Awards 1992

Our mission is simple: Every IDG book is designed to bring extra value and skill-building instructions to the reader. Our books are written by experts who understand and care about our readers. The knowledge base of our editorial staff comes from years of experience in publishing, education, and journalism — experience which we use to produce books for the '90s. In short, we care about books, so we attract the best people. We devote special attention to details such as audience, interior design, use of icons, and illustrations. And because we use an efficient process of authoring, editing, and desktop publishing our books electronically, we can spend more time ensuring superior content and spend less time on the technicalities of making books.

You can count on our commitment to deliver high-quality books at competitive prices on topics customers want to read about. At IDG, we value quality, and we have been delivering quality for more than 25 years. You'll find no better book on a subject than an IDG book.

John Kilcullen
President and CEO
IDG Books Worldwide, Inc.

WINNER
Ninth Annual Computer Press Awards 1993

IDG Books Worldwide, Inc., is a subsidiary of International Data Group. The officers are Patrick J. McGovern, Founder and Board Chairman; Walter Boyd, President. International Data Group's publications include: **ARGENTINA'S** Computerworld Argentina, Infoworld Argentina; **AUSTRALIA'S** Computerworld Australia, Australian PC World, Australian Macworld, Network World, Mobile Business Australia, Reseller, IDG Sources; **AUSTRIA'S** Computerwelt Oesterreich, PC Test; **BRAZIL'S** Computerworld, Gamepro, Game Power, Mundo IBM, Mundo Unix, PC World, Super Game; **BELGIUM'S** Data News (CW) **BULGARIA'S** Computerworld Bulgaria, Ediworld, PC & Mac World Bulgaria, Network World Bulgaria; **CANADA'S** CIO Canada, Computerworld Canada, Graduate Computerworld, InfoCanada, Network World Canada; **CHILE'S** Computerworld Chile, Informatica; **COLOMBIA'S** Computerworld Colombia, PC World; **CZECH REPUBLIC'S** Computerworld, Elektronika, PC World; **DENMARK'S** Communications World, Computerworld Danmark, Macintosh Produktkatalog, Macworld Danmark, PC World Danmark, PC World Produktguide, Tech World, Windows World; **ECUADOR'S** PC World Ecuador; **EGYPT'S** Computerworld (CW) Middle East, PC World Middle East; **FINLAND'S** MikroPC, Tietoviikko, Tietoverkko; **FRANCE'S** Distributique, GOLDEN MAC, InfoPC, Languages & Systems, Le Guide du Monde Informatique, Le Monde Informatique, Telecoms & Reseaux; **GERMANY'S** Computerwoche, Computerwoche Focus, Computerwoche Extra, Computerwoche Karriere, Information Management, Macwelt, Netzwelt, PC Welt, PC Woche, Publish, Unit; **GREECE'S** Infoworld, PC Games; **HUNGARY'S** Computerworld SZT, PC World; **HONG KONG'S** Computerworld Hong Kong, PC World Hong Kong; **INDIA'S** Computers & Communications; **IRELAND'S** ComputerScope; **ISRAEL'S** Computerworld Israel, PC World Israel; **ITALY'S** Computerworld Italia, Lotus Magazine, Macworld Italia, Networking Italia, PC Shopping, PC World Italia; **JAPAN'S** Computerworld Today, Information Systems World, Macworld Japan, Nikkei Personal Computing, SunWorld Japan, Windows World; **KENYA'S** East African Computer News; **KOREA'S** Computerworld Korea, Macworld Korea, PC World Korea; **MEXICO'S** Compu Edicion, Compu Manufactura, Computacion/Punto de Venta, Computerworld Mexico, MacWorld, Mundo Unix, PC World, Windows; **THE NETHERLANDS'** Computer! Totaal, Computable (CW), LAN Magazine, MacWorld, Totaal "Windows"; **NEW ZEALAND'S** Computer Listings, Computerworld New Zealand, New Zealand PC World, Network World; **NIGERIA'S** PC World Africa; **NORWAY'S** Computerworld Norge, C/World, Lotusworld Norge, Macworld Norge, Networld, PC World Ekspress, PC World Norge, PC World's Produktguide, Publish& Multimedia World, Student Data, Unix World, Windowsworld; IDG Direct Response; **PAKISTAN'S** PC World Pakistan; **PANAMA'S** PC World Panama; **PERU'S** Computerworld Peru, PC World; **PEOPLE'S REPUBLIC OF CHINA'S** China Computerworld, China Infoworld, Electronics Today/Multimedia World, Electronics International, Electronic Product World, China Network World, PC and Communications Magazine, PC World China, Software World Magazine, Telecom Product World; IDG HIGH TECH BEIJING'S New Product World; IDG SHENZHEN'S Computer News Digest; **PHILIPPINES'** Computerworld Philippines, PC Digest (PCW); **POLAND'S** Computerworld Poland, PC World/Komputer; **PORTUGAL'S** Cerebro/PC World, Correio Informatico/Computerworld, Informatica & Comunicacoes Catalogo, MacIn, Nacional de Produtos; **ROMANIA'S** Computerworld, PC World; **RUSSIA'S** Computerworld-Moscow, Mir - PC, Sety; **SINGAPORE'S** Computerworld Southeast Asia, PC World Singapore; **SLOVENIA'S** Monitor Magazine; **SOUTH AFRICA'S** Computer Mail (CIO),Computing S.A.,Network World S.A., Software World; **SPAIN'S** Advanced Systems, Amiga World, Computerworld Espana, Communicaciones World, Macworld Espana, NeXTWORLD, Super Juegos Magazine (GamePro), PC World Espana, Publish; **SWEDEN'S** Attack, ComputerSweden, Corporate Computing, Natverk & Kommunikation, Macworld, Mikrodatorn, PC World, Publishing & Design (CAP), Datalngenjoren, Maxi Data,Windows World; **SWITZERLAND'S** Computerworld Schweiz, Macworld Schweiz, PC Tip; **TAIWAN'S** Computerworld Taiwan, PC World Taiwan; **THAILAND'S** Thai Computerworld; **TURKEY'S** Computerworld Monitor, Macworld Turkiye, PC World Turkiye; **UKRAINE'S** Computerworld; **UNITED KINGDOM'S** Computing /Computerworld, Connexion/ Network World, Lotus Magazine, Macworld, Open Computing/Sunworld; **UNITED STATES'** Advanced Systems, AmigaWorld, Cable in the Classroom, CD Review, CIO, Computerworld, Digital Video, DOS Resource Guide, Electronic Entertainment Magazine, Federal Computer Week, Federal Integrator, GamePro, IDG Books, Infoworld, Infoworld Direct, Laser Event, Macworld, Multimedia World, Network World, PC Letter, PC World, PlayRight, Power PC World, Publish, SWATPro, Video Event; **VENEZUELA'S** Computerworld Venezuela, PC World; **VIETNAM'S** PC World Vietnam

Acknowledgments

The authors would like to thank Jordan Young, Lydia Spitzer, Meg Young, and T. H. Sophia for their support in writing this book.

In addition, we have enjoyed and appreciated the feedback we've gotten from readers of *The Internet For Dummies.* If you have comments about this book, be sure to e-mail us at `dummies@iecc.com`.

The publisher would like to give special thanks to Patrick J. McGovern, without whom this book would not have been possible.

Credits

VP & Publisher
David Solomon

Managing Editor
Mary Bednarek

Acquisitions Editor
Janna Custer

Production Director
Beth Jenkins

Senior Editors
Tracy L. Barr
Sandy Blackthorn
Diane Graves Steele

Production Coordinator
Cindy L. Phipps

Associate Acquisitions Editor
Megg Bonar

Editorial Assistant
Darlene Cunningham

Associate Project Editor
Corbin Collins

Editor
Shawn MacLaren

Technical Reviewer
William Coy Hatfield

Production Staff
Tony Augsburger
Valery Bourke
Mary Breidenbach
Chris Collins
Sherry Gomoll
Drew R. Moore
Kathie Schnorr
Gina Scott

Proofreader
Charles A. Hutchinson

Indexer
Sharon Hilgenberg

Conventions

Because the Internet is made of so many different kinds of systems, computers, software, commands, and so forth, this book uses different typefaces and other tricks to mean different things and to (hopefully) clarify stuff.

In a paragraph of regular text, sometimes we tell you to type something — whatever you are to type appears in bold: **like this.** Be sure to type it just as it appears. Use the same capitalization as we do that because sometimes the Internet — in particular, the UNIX parts of it — considers uppercase and lowercase versions of the same letter to be totally different beasts.

Filenames, host names, Internet programs, and commands are presented in a special typeface: `like this.`

Information that you provide appears in italic: *like this.* For example, if you see something like *yourname* or *your.computer's.name,* fill in those parts with the actual information.

Sometimes, we describe something that is (or should be) happening on your screen. Things that happen on-screen appear separated from the regular text:

```
Cryptic Internet stuff that pops up on your
screen looks like this.

Sometimes, stuff appears on your screen, and
you have to type something.

In that case, the thing you are to type ap-
pears in bold: like this.
```

Don't worry, it'll become clearer as you go along.

Contents at a Glance

Introduction

At last — an Internet reference book that includes only the services and options you might conceivably have some interest in! In this book, you'll find information about lots of Internet services — over a dozen — along with how to use them. But we've left out a million boring features and warts that only nerds love.

How to find things in this book

It's divided into seven sections so you can find things fast:

- Part 1, "Internet Basics," contains information on connecting to the Internet and network names and addresses.
- Part 2, "Electronic Mail," discusses how to send, receive, file, answer, discard, and otherwise deal with the electronic lifeblood of the Net.
- Part 3, "Network News," tells you how Usenet news can help you stay in touch, answer questions, and waste incredible amounts of time.
- Part 4, "On-Line Communication," shows you how to use the Net to find out about and chat with people *right now*!
- Part 5, "Moving Files," covers transferring files, particularly from one of the thousands of public repositories to your own computer where you can use them.
- Part 6, "Finding Resources," explores on-line features that can help you find the locations of the resources you want.
- Part 7, "Interactive Information Facilities," shows you modern, way-cool network facilities that help you search and retrieve material with amazing ease.

What the icons mean

For each task or command, we include the following icons:

Easy for just about anyone to use.

Requires some attention and care and/or can be somewhat tricky.

Requires full attention and care and/or is very tricky.

Points out stuff you'll want to remember.

A tip that can save you time or impress your local Internaut.

Watch out for this! Something about this can make trouble for you.

A tip on where to find something on the Net — usually flags Internet addresses where you can get stuff.

A handy cross-reference to the sections in *The Internet For Dummies* that cover this topic in more detail.

Points out references to other places in this book where you can learn more about the topic at hand.

Part 1

Internet Basics

Before you can do anything interesting on the Internet, you need a few basic items. Specifically, you need some sort of hookup to the Net and an idea of the names of the things you want to use. This Part deals with basics such as connection, names, numbers, protocols, and zones.

Accessing the Internet

Connecting your computer to the Internet so that you can use its services.

You can connect to the Internet in several different ways. The services available on the Net are pretty much the same regardless of how you connect.

Direct connection

If you work at an organization whose computer networks are connected to the Internet, your computer is *on the Net,* and you can use Internet facilities directly.

UNIX workstations: If you're using a UNIX workstation, you're probably ready to start networking, because network software is a standard part of the UNIX system.

PCs and Macs: If you're using a PC or a Mac, you may have to do some configuration work — in fact, you may even have to install network hardware and software. Talk to your network administrator to find out what you must do.

See *The Internet For Dummies*, Chapter 3, "Starting Off, If You're a DOS User," for DOS hints; Chapter 4, "Starting Off, If You're a UNIX User," for UNIX workstation hints; and Chapter 5, "Starting Off, for Everyone Else," for Macintosh hints. Also see Chapter 28, "Sources of Internet Software," for advice on getting DOS and Mac Internet network software.

SLIP and PPP: dial-up networking

It's possible to use a dial-up connection as a network link so that your computer is considered to be on the Internet during the time you are connected on-line. The two schemes used for dial-up links are

- SLIP (Serial Line Internet Protocol)
- PPP (Point to Point Protocol)

Some organizations use SLIP or PPP to connect PCs or Macs to the Internet, whereas others use a SLIP link to connect the local network to the outside world. In the former case, it's up to you to start up and shut down the connection; in the latter case, the connection is made on demand or when scheduled.

See *The Internet For Dummies*, Chapter 3, section "SLIP sliding away." Some public Internet service providers offer SLIP service — see Chapter 27, "Public Internet Service Providers," for more information. See Chapter 28 for information about software.

Terminal dial-up

You can use a terminal or a PC running a terminal program to dial into a public Internet service provider. After you're connected, you can access whatever services the provider offers. The provider usually charges a set fee for these services, either per month or per connect hour.

See *The Internet For Dummies*, Chapter 27, "Public Internet Service Providers," for a list of providers and their phone numbers.

Communications Protocols

Methods that computers use to talk to each other.

The Internet has an endless list of communications protocols. In case you need to communicate (in English or Geek-speak) with an

Internet guru, the following table lists some of the more important protocols:

Protocol	What It Is
IP (Internet Protocol)	The underlying protocol used to pass data from one Internet host to another.
TCP (Transport Control Protocol)	Used for applications that need a continuing connection between two computers, such as remote login. Always used in connection with IP; often known as TCP/IP.
UDP (User Datagram Protocol)	Parallel to TCP, used for applications that send one-shot messages to each other.
SMTP (Simple Mail Transfer Protocol)	Misnamed protocol used to transfer e-mail from one host to another.
ARP (Address Resolution Protocol)	Specialized protocol used to identify hosts on an Ethernet local network.
ICMP (Internet Control Message Protocol)	Used to pass control and error messages.
FTP (File Transfer Protocol)	Used by the `ftp` program to transfer files from one host to another.

See *The Internet For Dummies*, Chapter 6, sections "Defining the Internet" and "TCP: The Rocket-Powered Mailman."

Host Names

Names given to Internet hosts.

Hosts are machines that are directly attached to the Internet — as opposed to those machines only connected indirectly for e-mail.

Host names have several parts strung together with periods, like

```
xuxa.iecc.com
```

You decode a host name from right to left. The rightmost part of a name is its *zone* (in the example, `com`). To the zone's left (`iecc`) is the name of the company, school, or organization. The part left of the company name identifies the particular machine within the organization. In large organizations, host names are further subdivided by site or department.

A partial name is known as a *domain*. For example, `xuxa` is in the `iecc.com` and `com` domains.

On the Internet, not all names are created equal. In particular, many names are valid only for mail.

Host Numbers

Numbers assigned to Internet hosts.

Network software uses the host number, which is sort of like a phone number, to identify the host. Host numbers are written in four chunks separated by periods, such as

```
140.186.81.6
```

Host numbers consist of two parts:

- The *network number* indicates the network that a host is connected to.
- The *local host number* identifies the particular computer on the network.

The network number comprises the first one, two, or three chunks, depending on the first chunk. The rest of the host number is the local host number, as shown in the following table:

Class Number	First Chunk	Length of Network	Maximum No. Hosts on Network
A	1–126	1 chunk	16,387,064
B	128–191	2 chunks	64,516
C	192–223	3 chunks	254

Sample

What does host number 140.186.81.6 mean? The first chunk (140) means that it is a Class B network; the network number, therefore, is in two parts: network 140.186, host 81.6.

There is no particular relationship between host names and host numbers. A computer can have a host number but no host name — for example, a computer used by other computers but not by humans — and it can have multiple host numbers if it's connected to multiple networks.

The most important computer number to know is the host number of the computer you use, for two reasons:

- A few systems on the Internet, notably those run by the U.S. military, don't handle names very well, so some users may need your number to contact you.

- If things get fouled up, the number will help the guru who fixes your problem.

See *The Internet For Dummies*, Chapter 2, section "What's in a Number?"

Port Numbers

Numbers that identify the program that a host computer uses to connect to the Internet.

Internet hosts usually can run many programs at once, and they can have simultaneous network connections to lots of other computers. The different connections are kept straight by *port numbers*, which identify particular programs on a computer. For example, file transfer uses port 21, e-mail uses port 25, and network news uses port 119.

Most of the time, programs automatically select the correct port to use. Now and then, though, a service will use a nonstandard port. In this book, when we describe a service that uses a nonstandard port, we tell you the port number.

See *The Internet For Dummies*, Chapter 6, section "Any Port in a Storm."

Zones

The last two or three letters in a host name.

There are two main kinds of zones:

- Organizational names
- Geographic names

Organizational names

If the zone is three letters long, it is an *organizational name*. The three-letter code indicates the type of organization, and the part just before the zone indicates the specific organization.

Although organizational names don't tell you anything about a system's physical location, most systems that use organizational names are in the United States. The following table describes currently used organizational names.

Zone	Type of Organization
com	Commercial organization
edu	Educational institution
gov	Government body or department
int	International organization (mostly NATO, at the moment)
mil	Military site
net	Networking organization
org	Anything that doesn't fit elsewhere, such as a professional society

See *The Internet For Dummies*, Chapter 2, section "The Twilight Zone?"

Geographic names

If the zone is two letters long, it is a *geographic name*. The two-letter code specifies a country, and the stuff in front of the zone is specific to the country. The us domain, used by some schools and small organizations in the United States, is set up strictly geographically. For example, my machine in Cambridge, Massachusetts, is called chico.iecc.cambridge.ma.us.

Note: A host can have more than one name. My machine is also known as chico.iecc.com.

The following table lists popular geographic names.

Zone	Country
at	Austria, Republic of
be	Belgium, Kingdom of
br	Brazil, Federative Republic of
ca	Canada
fr	France (French Republic)
jp	Japan
mx	Mexico (United Mexican States)
nl	Netherlands, Kingdom of the
no	Norway, Kingdom of
ru	Russian Federation
es	Spain, Kingdom of
se	Sweden, Kingdom of
ch	Switzerland (Swiss Confederation)
uk	United Kingdom (official code is gb but uk commonly used)
us	United States of America

See *The Internet For Dummies*, Chapter 2, section “Where’s Vanuatu?”

For a complete list of country codes, see Appendix A of this book, “Internet Connections by Country.”

Other zones

You may encounter a few other zones, including the following:

`arpa` Left over from the ARPANET, the Internet’s predecessor

`bitnet` Pseudozone used for mail to BITNET (another network)

`uucp` Pseudozone used for mail to sites that use *uucp,* a crusty old network that uses dial-up modems

Part 2

Electronic Mail

Electronic mail, or *e-mail,* is without a doubt the most widely used Internet service. Every system on the Net supports some sort of mail service (except for special systems that are not used by humans). In other words, no matter what kind of computer you use, if it's on the Internet, you can send and receive mail.

Mail programs (or *mailers*) enable you to read and send mail as well as store messages for later reference. People with UNIX workstations on the Internet, in fact, use at least a dozen different mail programs. Still more mail programs are used on the other kinds of computers attached directly and indirectly to the Net. Users of on-line services such as MCI Mail, CompuServe, and America Online can exchange mail with the Internet using the standard mailers provided with those services.

Three popular UNIX-based mailers are

- Berkeley mail (usually called `mail`, sometimes called `Mail` or `mailx`)
- `elm`, a mailer with a full-screen terminal interface — all HP workstations come with `elm`
- `xmail`, a graphic mailer that runs on the X Window system (deep down, `xmail` is really Berkeley mail only with a prettier face)

Each of these mail programs lets you read your incoming mail, send new mail, reply to messages you receive, forward messages to other people, and save messages for later. This part covers how to work with these big three mail programs.

Much more than any other Internet service, mail is connected to many non-Internet mail systems. See the section "Sending Mail to Non-Internet Systems" in this Part.

For more information on e-mail, see *The Internet For Dummies*, Chapter 7, "Basics of Electronic Mail" or *UNIX For Dummies*, Chapter 18, "Automating Your Office Gossip."

Addresses

Codes that specify where Internet mail messages should be sent.

Roughly speaking, mail addresses consist of

- Mailbox name
- @ (*at* sign)
- Host name

For example, `elvis@ntw.org` is a typical address, where `elvis` is the mailbox name and `ntw.org` is the host name.

The rules for host names are described in Part 1 (see the section "Host Names").

Internet mailbox names can contain letters, numerals, and punctuation such as periods and underscores but *not* commas, spaces, or parentheses.

If you must send mail to an address that *does* include commas, spaces, or parentheses, enclose the address in "double quotes."

What's my address?

Most likely, your address is this: *your.login.name@your.computer's.name.*

However, system administrators can make mail addresses be anything they want. For example, a host name often is just a department or company name rather than your computer's name. If your login name is `elvis`, and your computer is `shamu.strat.ntw.org`, your mail address may be `elvis@shamu.strat.ntw.org`, `elvis@strat.ntw.org`, or `elvis@ntw.org`. (You can have multiple addresses, so all three addresses may work!)

Because it can be hard to remember everyone's login name, many organizations create mail addresses based on people's real names, such as `elvis.presley@ntw.org`.

If you're using a computer such as a PC or a Mac that doesn't require you to log in, your mail is probably handled by a *central mail server.* As a result, you should use your login name — that is, the name you use when you contact the mail server.

If you're not sure what your mail address is, send e-mail to Internet For Dummies Central at `iqdummies@iecc.com`, and we'll send back a note containing the address from which your message was sent, which is your mail address. While you're at it, add a sentence or two telling us whether you like this book.

See *The Internet For Dummies*, Chapter 7, section "What's My Address?"

Forwarding Messages in Berkeley Mail

Sending a copy of an incoming message to a third party using the Berkeley mail program.

1. After you read a message, press **m** to tell the program that you want to create a new message.

   (For how to read an e-mail message, see the sections "Reading Mail..." in this Part.)
2. Type the address to which you want to forward the message.
3. Enter an appropriate `Subject:` when asked.
4. Type **~m** on a separate line to insert the original message.
5. Enter more text if you want. Then type a period on a separate line to end your message.

   The program responds with `EOT` (End of Text). ***Note:*** In some old versions of `mail`, typing a period doesn't work. Press Ctrl-D instead.

See *The Internet For Dummies*, Chapter 8, section "Truth in forwarding."

Forwarding Messages in `elm`

Sending a copy of an incoming message to a third party using the `elm` mail program.

`elm` lets you send copies of a message to one or more people.

1. Run `elm`.
2. Display the message on your screen.
3. Press **f** to forward the message.

   `elm` asks whether you want to edit the message as you forward it.

4. Press **y** or **n**.

   `elm` asks where you want the message forwarded to.

5. Type the address.

6. Edit the message (unless, of course, you said that you didn't want to) and then send it the same way you would send a new message.

See *The Internet For Dummies*, Chapter 8, section "Truth in forwarding."

Forwarding Messages in xmail

Sending a copy of an incoming message to a third party using the `xmail` mail program.

1. Run `xmail` if it is not already running or double-click on its icon if it is.

2. Display the message you want to forward.

3. Hold down Shift and click on the Send button.

4. Edit and send the message the same way as a new message. `xmail` provides the `Subject:` after you edit the message and then lets you type in the recipient's address.

See *The Internet For Dummies*, Chapter 8, section "Truth in forwarding."

Mail Etiquette

Generally accepted rules of polite e-mail communication.

It's easy to send electronic mail that seems rude or obnoxious, even when you don't mean to. Here are a few suggestions regarding mail style:

- *Don't flame.* That is, don't send messages full of pointless and excessive outrage.

- *Watch your tone.* E-mail can inadvertently seem brusque or rude.

- *Double-check your humor.* Irony and sarcasm are easy to miss and can come across as annoying or dumb instead. Sometimes, it helps to add a *smiley*, like this one `:-)` to say clearly, "This is a joke."

- *Remember that e-mail is not particularly private.* A glitch can cause the system to deliver your mail to the wrong recipient on the wrong system.
- *Don't pass on chain letters.* In particular, don't pass on the one about the dying boy who wants greeting cards (he doesn't), the "modem tax" rumor (the proposal was squelched in 1987), or the letter from Dave Rhodes that offers you a way to make money fast (it's illegal and doesn't work).

See *The Internet For Dummies*, Chapter 7, section "A Few Words from the Etiquette Ladies" and Chapter 8, sidebar "Chain letters: Arrrrrggghhh!"

Mail Headers

Header lines that appear at the beginning of every mail message.

You can edit mail headers before sending the message:

- In Berkeley mail, type **~h** while typing in the message.
- In `elm`, press **h** after editing the message.
- In `xmail`, type the new header in the form displayed after you edit the message.

Some mail headers are required, some are recommended, and some are optional — as shown in the following table:

Header	Description
`Subject:`	Describes message (recommended)
`To:`	Lists recipient(s) of the message (required)
`Cc:`	Lists carbon copy recipient(s) (optional)
`Bcc:`	Lists blind carbon copy recipient(s), not sent with message (optional)
`From:`	Address of message author (required, provided automatically)
`Reply-To:`	Address to send replies to if different than `From:` (optional)
`Date:`	Time and date message sent (required, provided automatically)
`Expires:`	Date after which message expires (optional)

Header	Description
`Message-ID:`	Unique machine-generated identifier for message (required, provided automatically)
`Lines:`	Number of lines of text in message (optional, provided automatically)

Note: Various other optional header lines exist (but none of great importance).

Mailing Lists — Basics

Lists of e-mail addresses.

A *mailing list* offers a way for a group of people with a shared interest to send messages to each other and hold a group conversation. A mailing list has a mail address, and (more or less) anything that someone sends to that address is sent to all the people on the list. People on the list often respond to the messages, resulting in a running conversation.

For groups of more than a few hundred people, a network newsgroup is preferable — see Part 3, "Network News."

Addresses of mailing lists

Actually, every mailing list has *two* mail addresses:

- *The list address.* Messages sent to this address are forwarded to all the addresses on the list. The mailing list's address thus works like a broadcasting service. Therefore, only send messages to this address that you want hundreds of people to read.

  Do not use the mailing list address for administrative matters, such as unsubscribing from the list.

- *The request address (or manager's address).* Messages sent to this address are read only by the list manager. Use this address for messages about subscribing and unsubscribing. Messages to this address may be read by a computer, in which case you may need to put them in a specific format.

See the section "Mailing Lists — Getting On and Off" in this Part.

Naming conventions of lists

Two naming conventions exist for the two addresses of a mailing list:

* For lists that are maintained manually, add **-request** to the list's address to get the request address.

  For example, if a list is named `unicycles@blivet.com`, the request address is almost certainly `unicycles-request@blivet.com`.

* For lists that are maintained automatically, the request address is usually **LISTSERV@** followed by the name of the host where the list is maintained.

  For example, LISTSERV@blivet.com. A few systems use a mailing list package called majordomo in which case the address would be something like `majordomo@blivet.com`.

Mailing Lists — Getting On and Off

Adding or removing your e-mail address to or from a mailing list.

For lists maintained manually

Send a mail message (like "Please add me to the unicycles list" or "Please remove me from the unicycles list") to the request address. The messages are read by humans, so no fixed form is required. Be sure to include your real name and be polite and brief.

For lists maintained automatically

Send the request to the LISTSERV or majordomo address. The subscription request must take the following fixed form:

```
sub listname yourname
```

where `sub` is short for subscribe, *listname* is the name of the mailing list you want to be on, and *yourname* is your real name. You don't need to include your e-mail address because it is automatically included as your message's return address.

For example, to subscribe to the unicycles mailing list, send this message (if your name is Roger Sherman):

```
sub unicycles Roger Sherman
```

To get off the list, send this message to the LISTSERV or majordomo address:

```
signoff unicycles
```

Your e-mail address and real name aren't required because LISTSERV and majordomo already know them.

More stuff

When subscribing to a list maintained by LISTSERV or majordomo, be sure to send your `sub` message from the computer where you want mail messages sent. Remember: they use your message's return address as the address they add to the mailing list.

Be sure to send requests to get on and off the list to the *request* address, not to the list itself.

See *The Internet For Dummies*, Chapter 10, section "Getting on and off mailing lists."

Mailing Lists — Receiving Messages

Receiving messages from mailing lists you have joined.

As soon as you join a list, you automatically receive all messages from the list along with the rest of your mail.

Some lists are available in *digest* form with all the day's messages combined with a table of contents. Often, LISTSERV systems can send either a digest or individual messages. To get the digest for the unicycles mailing list, if available, send this message to the LISTSERV address:

```
set unicycle digest
```

See *The Internet For Dummies*, Chapter 10, sidebar "Urrp! Computer's Digest Messages!" and section "Stupid LISTSERV tricks."

Mailing Lists — Sending Messages

Sending messages to mailing lists you have joined.

To send a message to a mailing list, just mail a message to the list's address. The message is automatically distributed to the list's members. Some lists are moderated — in other words, a human being screens the messages before sending them, which can delay the messages by up to a day or two.

LISTSERV systems usually send you copies of your own messages to confirm that they were received. You can tell LISTSERV not to return (*acknowledge*) your own messages by sending the following message to the unicycles mailing list's LISTSERV address:

```
set unicycles noack
```

To resume receiving copies of your own messages, send

```
set unicycles ack
```

See *The Internet For Dummies*, Chapter 10, section "Sending Messages to Mailing Lists."

2

Notification of Arriving Mail

When mail arrives, your system may try to tell you about it. Some systems announce "You have mail!" — others boop and beep. If a mail icon is on your screen, it may change its appearance.

Reading Mail in Berkeley Mail

Reading your e-mail messages using the Berkeley `mail` program.

Berkeley mail is not a particularly friendly environment for reading mail. Why not ask your system administrator to install `elm`?

1. Run the `mail` program. `mail` lists your messages, marking the new ones with an angle bracket.
2. Press Enter to see the first message.

   After you read the message, you can discard it, reply to it, forward it, or file it. If you don't tell the program what to do with a message, the mailer either leaves the message in your mailbox or saves it to a file called `mbox`.
3. To delete the message and move to the next, type **dp** (Delete and Print) and then press Enter. To go to the next message without deleting the current one, just press Enter.
4. To leave Berkeley mail, press **q** to finalize your changes (if you deleted any messages) and quit or press **x** to exit without deleting anything.

If your mailer automatically saves messages in `mbox`, be sure to review and delete unneeded messages in your mailbox at least once a week.

A few totally antique mailers immediately show you the first message. If this happens to you, demand better software. (These mailers are predecessors of Berkeley mail from about 1979. Sheesh.)

You can see the `Subject:` lines of your messages again by pressing **h**. To pick a message from the list, type the number shown on the line with the message.

Reading Mail in elm

A friendly, easy way to read your mail.

Using `elm`, after you read your messages, you can delete them, stash them in folders for later use, or forward them to unsuspecting recipients.

1. Run `elm`. It lists your incoming messages, marking new ones with an `N`.
2. Press Enter to see the first new message. If the message is more than one screen long, press the spacebar to see each subsequent screen.
3. Press **d** to delete the current message and go on to the next. Or when viewing the last (or only) screen of the message, press the spacebar to go on to the next message without deleting the current one.
4. To leave `elm`, press **q** to finalize your changes (if you deleted any messages) and quit or press **x** to exit without deleting anything. Either way, `elm` may ask you to confirm your choice. If it does, press **y** to go ahead and **n** not to.

You can see the list of `Subject:` lines again by pressing **i** (for index). To pick a message from the list, type the number shown on the line with the message. Or use the up- and down-arrow keys to move to the message and then press Enter to see the message.

Reading Mail in xmail

Reading your mail using the `xmail` program (which allows the use of a mouse).

1. Run `xmail` if it is not already running or double-click its icon if it is.

   `xmail` should show the first new message in the bottom part of the window. If it doesn't, click on the Newmail button to make the program look for new mail. The subject lines of new messages appear marked with an *N* in the upper part of the `xmail` window.

2. If the message doesn't fit in the window, click in the gray bar to the left of the message to scroll through the message.
3. To delete the current message, click on the Delete button.
4. To go to the next message, hold down Shift and click on the Read button.
5. To leave `xmail`, click on the Quit button. To hide `xmail` under its icon (or *iconize* it), which is preferable unless you're about to log out, click on the little blob in the upper left-hand corner of the `xmail` window.

The list (or index) of messages and their `Subject:` lines appears in the top half of the `xmail` window. You can click the left and right mouse buttons in the bar to the left of the index to scroll up and down. To pick a message from the list, click on the desired line in the index and then click on the Read button to see the message.

See *The Internet For Dummies*, Chapter 7, section "Mail Call!"

Reading Messages in a Mailbox Using Berkeley Mail

Rereading messages that you previously saved in a mailbox or folder in the Berkeley mail program.

Run the `mail` program using the `-f` option on the command line, like this:

```
Mail -f oldmail
```

Replace `Mail` with the name your system gives to Berkeley mail (usually `mail` or `Mail`) and `oldmail` with the name of your mailbox.

Reading Messages in a Mailbox Using `elm`

Rereading messages that you previously saved in a mailbox or folder in the `elm` mail program.

You can also ask `elm` to show you a list of the mailboxes (which it calls *folders*) that you have created.

1. Run elm.
2. Press **c** (for Change mailbox).

   elm asks for the name of the mailbox.
3. Enter the name of the mailbox.
4. elm shows you a list of the messages in the mailbox. You can read them, reply to them, and so on just as if they were incoming messages.
5. To switch back to the list of incoming messages, press **c** again. When elm asks for the mailbox name, press **!**. elm may ask whether you want to save changes to the old mailbox (press **y** or **n**).

Another way to tell elm to show you the messages in a particular mailbox is to use the -f option on the command line, like so:

```
elm -f oldmail
```

Replace oldmail with the name of your mailbox.

You can ask elm to show you a list of the *folders* (or mailboxes) you have created in your Mail directory by pressing **?** when elm asks for a folder name. When you change to or save to a mailbox, prefix the name of the mailbox with an equal sign (=) to tell elm to put the mailbox in your Mail directory rather than the current directory (usually your login directory).

Reading Messages in a Mailbox Using xmail

Rereading messages that you previously saved in a mailbox or folder in the xmail program (use the Folder button).

1. Run xmail if it is not already running or double-click its icon if it is. Using the mouse, move the cursor to the File: area in the center of the screen.
2. Type the name of the mailbox you want to use.
3. Click on the Folder button.

Replying to Messages Using Berkeley Mail

Sending a message back to someone who wrote to you.

Because the `mail` program can automatically address your reply, it's easier to respond to a message than to type a new one.

1. After you read a mail message, press **r** to tell the program that you want to reply.

   `mail` creates a new message addressed to the sender of the original message. The new message has the same subject as the original message.

2. Type the text of your reply the same way you enter a new message. Then type a period on a separate line to end your message.

   The program responds with `EOT` (End of Text). ***Note:*** In some old versions of `mail`, typing a period doesn't work. Press Ctrl-D instead.

See *The Internet For Dummies,* Chapter 8, section "Truth in Forwarding."

Replying to Messages Using `elm`

Sending a message back to someone who wrote to you.

1. Run `elm`.
2. Display the message on your screen.
3. Press **r** to reply to the message.
4. `elm` asks whether to include a copy of the original message (which you can edit) into your reply. Press **y** or **n**.
5. Edit the message and send the reply the same way you would a new message.

See *The Internet For Dummies,* Chapter 8, section "Truth in Forwarding."

Replying to Messages Using `xmail`

Sending a message back to someone who wrote to you.

1. Run `xmail` if it is not already running or double-click on its icon if it is.
2. Display the message to which you want to reply.
3. Click on the Reply button. If you want to include the original message in the reply text, hold down Shift while clicking on Reply.

4. Edit and send the message the same way as a new message. `xmail` provides the subject and recipient address automatically after you edit the message.

See *The Internet For Dummies,* Chapter 8, section "Truth in Forwarding."

Saving Messages Using Berkeley Mail or elm

Saving incoming mail messages for later use by storing them in a *mailbox* or *folder.*

1. Display the message on screen.
2. Press **s** (for save).
3. Type the name of a mailbox (or folder).
4. `elm` suggests a mailbox name based on the sender's name. Press Enter to accept the suggestion, or type another name and then press Enter.

See *The Internet For Dummies*, Chapter 8, section "Cold potatoes."

Saving Messages Using xmail

Saving incoming mail messages for later use by storing them in a *mailbox.*

1. Display the message you want to save.
2. Using the mouse, move the cursor to the `File:` area in the center of the screen.
3. Type the name of the mailbox.
4. Click on the Save button.

See *The Internet For Dummies*, Chapter 8, section "Cold potatoes."

Sending Mail to Non-Internet Systems

Sending e-mail to people on non-Internet networks or mail systems, such as CompuServe, America Online, or MCI Mail.

Many systems and networks that are not directly connected to the Internet nevertheless have a mail connection. The following table lists how to address messages to non-Internet mail connections, where *username* is the name that the recipient uses to log on, *usernum* is the recipient's numerical user ID, and *hostname* is the name of the particular computer within the network.

System	*How to Address Messages*
America Online	*username*@aol.com
AT&T Mail	*username*@attmail.com
BITNET	*username*@hostname.bitnet or *username%hostname*.bitnet@mitvma.mit.edu or *username%hostname*.bitnet@cunyvm.cuny.edu
BIX	*username*@bix.com
CompuServe	*userid.userid*@compuserve.com *userid.userid* is the numerical CompuServe ID with a period replacing the comma. For example, if the person's CompuServe ID is 71234,567, send mail to 71234.567@compuserve.com.
Delphi	*username@delphi.com*
Easylink	*userid*@eln.attmail.com *userid* is the seven-digit user ID number.
FIDOnet	*firstname.lastname*@p4.f3.n2.z1.fidonet.org or *firstname.lastname*@f3.n2.z1.fidonet.org Replace the numbers with parts of the person's FIDO node number. For example, this user's FIDO node number would be 1:2/3.4 or 1:2/3.
GEnie	*mailname*@genie.geis.com *mailname* is based on the user's name, not the user's random login access name.
MCI Mail	*usernum*@mcimail.com *usernum* is the person's numerical MCI mail address, usually written in the form 123-4567. Leave out the hyphen, though.
Prodigy	*usernum*@prodigy.com ***Note:*** The person's Prodigy account must be set up for Internet mail.
Sprintmail	/G=*firstname*/S=*lastname*/O=*orgname*/C=US/ADMD=TELEMAIL/@sprint.com
UUCP	*username@hostname*.uucp or *hostname*!*username*@internet_gateway ***Note:*** The first UUCP form works only for registered addresses. The most common gateway is uunet.uu.net.

See *The Internet For Dummies*, Chapter 9, section "A Parade of Mail Systems."

Sending Mail Using Berkeley Mail

Not a particularly friendly program for sending mail, but it works.

1. Run the `mail` program, entering the address to which you want to send your message.

   For example, type **mail king@ntw.com.**

2. Enter an appropriate subject if `mail` asks you for a `Subject:` line. If it does not, you should enter a `Subject:` line anyway by typing **~s** followed by the subject.

3. Type your message, using as many lines as necessary.

4. End your message by typing a period on a line by itself.

   The program responds with `EOT` (End of text). ***Note:*** In some old versions of `mail`, typing a period doesn't work. Press Ctrl-D instead.

If you change your mind and decide not to send a message, press the interrupt character (usually Ctrl-C or Del) three times to make `mail` give up.

See *The Internet For Dummies*, Chapter 7, section "Ahoy, there" or *UNIX For Dummies*, Chapter 18, section "Playing Postman Pat with `mail`."

Sending Mail Using `elm`

A very nice program for sending mail.

1. Run `elm`.

   `elm`'s main screen lists your incoming messages and displays a menu of commands. Press **m** to send a message. Alternatively, you can give `elm` the recipient's address when you run it. For example, you can type **elm king@ntw.com**.

2. `elm` asks you to enter a `Subject:`. Type one and press Enter.

3. `elm` may ask for `Copies to:`. Type any addresses to which you want to send copies of the message and press Enter.

4. elm runs the standard local text editor, usually vi or emacs. Type the message, save the file, and exit the editor.

   elm comes back with a little menu, like this:

   ```
   Choose e)dit message, !)shell, h)eaders,
   c)opy file, s)end, or f)orget.
   ```

5. Press **s** to send the message. Press **f** if you don't want to send it.

6. elm responds with a cheery Mail sent! and then returns to the list of your incoming messages and a menu of commands.

   Note: If you started elm with the recipient's name on the command line, at this point elm just exits.

   To exit from elm, press **q**. elm may ask you to confirm your choice. If so, press **y** to go ahead and **n** not to.

The pine mail program acts like a simplified elm; you send and read mail the same way.

See *The Internet For Dummies*, Chapter 7, section "Ahoy, there" or *UNIX For Dummies*, Chapter 18, section "Playing Postman Pat with elm." For information on using the vi or emacs text editors, see *UNIX For Dummies*, Chapter 12, "Writing Deathless Prose."

Sending Mail Using Other Mail Programs

Sending mail using some program other than Berkeley mail, elm, or xmail.

Details vary, but the steps generally echo those outlined in the sections in this Part that deal with those three programs. In general, you do the following:

1. Tell your mailer that you want to send a message.
2. Enter the address.
3. Enter the message and subject.
4. Tell the program that you're done.

See *The Internet For Dummies*, Chapter 7, section "What if I have some other kind of computer?"

If you're using a personal computer of some sort, your incoming mail may be stored on a central machine called a *mail server* rather than be delivered to your PC automatically. In that case, you usually have to tell the mail program on the PC to fetch your new mail from the central machine before you can read it. The commands to do so vary considerably, unfortunately, so you need to get local advice.

Many networked PCs run a commercial mail system such as cc:Mail or Microsoft Mail rather than an Internet mailer. These systems don't directly connect to the Internet. It is often possible, however, to send messages to Internet mail addresses by using a special address of some sort. Again, get local advice.

See *The Internet For Dummies*, Chapter 7, sidebar "Are PCs real computers, mailwise?"

Sending Mail Using xmail

A nice, user-friendly way to send e-mail.

1. Run `xmail`. Click on the Send button (in the middle of the screen).

   `xmail` creates a new window, which runs the standard local text editor, such as `vi` or `emacs`.

2. Type your message, save the file, and leave the editor.

   `xmail` pops up another window.

3. Type the address(es) to which you want to send the message and then press Enter.

4. Type the message's subject. Add `Cc:` and `Bcc:` addresses if you so desire.

5. Click on Deliver to send the message.

If you don't want to send the message, hold down Ctrl while you click on Deliver. `xmail` discards the message.

See *The Internet For Dummies*, Chapter 7, section "Ahoy, there." For information on using the `vi` or `emacs` text editors, see *UNIX For Dummies*, Chapter 12, "Writing Deathless Prose."

Part 3

Network News

Network news, also known as *Usenet,* also known as *net news,* is a gigantic worldwide distributed bulletin board system. Users around the world, using thousands of host computers, enter Usenet messages, and within a day or so the messages are delivered to nearly every other Usenet host (probably including yours) for everyone to read.

Over 30,000 news articles — comprising over 50 megabytes of text — slosh through Usenet every day, so it can be a big challenge to pick out the parts you're interested in.

See Appendix B for an extensive list of newsgroups.

Extracting Binary Files

Transforming encoded binary files back into their original forms.

Some files contain encoded binary data, such as pictures or executable programs. Such messages look like this:

```
begin plugh.exe 644
M390GNM4L-REP3PT45G00I-05[I5-6M30ME,MRMK760PI5LPTMETLMKPY
ME0T39I4905B05Y0PV30IXKRTL5KWLJR0JT0U,6P5;3;MRU050I4J50I4
```

(This is called *uuencoded* format.)

Before you can use this information, you must *extract* it.

1. Press **e** followed by Enter. If you want the data someplace other than your News directory, type the directory name after the **e**.
2. If the file is large and is split across multiple messages, press **e** in each of the messages in order.

Extracting Groups of Files

Transforming an encoded group of binary files back into their original forms.

Some messages contain groups of files — most often a group of C program files in *shar* (shell archive) format. Extract them with `e` in exactly the same way as binary files (see preceding section).

See *The Internet For Dummies*, Chapter 11, section "Honest, it's a work of art."

Finding a Newsgroup

Locating a newsgroup on your news reader.

To read the messages of a particular newsgroup, use the `g` (*goto*) command.

1. Press **g**.
2. Type the name of the newsgroup.
3. Press Enter.

   Your news reader subscribes you to the newsgroup.

Note: If you have unsubscribed to a group and want to turn it back on, the `g` command turns it back on.

Junking and Killing Uninteresting Articles

Means just what it says.

Often, you find an article to be uninteresting enough that you want to skip it, all the replies, and perhaps every future reply as well.

- To skip (kill) this article and all others with the same subject, press **k** (lowercase).
- To curse this subject permanently and skip it in the future as well, press **K** (uppercase).
- To skip (junk) the rest of this thread, even if the subject changes, press **J** (uppercase).

See *The Internet For Dummies*, Chapter 11, sidebars "Arrgh! it's a kill file" and "Don't say I didn't warn you."

Leaving the News Reader

Exiting your news reader program.

When you are bored with reading messages from computer nerds all over world, or when you realize that it's almost five o'clock and you haven't gotten any useful work done all day, it's time to exit from your news reader.

1. Press **q**.
2. Depending on where you are in the program, you may have to press **q** two or three times.

New Newsgroups

Because Usenet is still growing like crazy, new newsgroups appear several times a week. Each time you run `rn` or `trn`, if any new newsgroups have appeared, you have the opportunity to subscribe to them.

1. Run `trn` or `rn`. It asks a question like this:

   ```
   Checking active list for new newsgroups...
   ```

   ```
   Newsgroup alt.comp.hardware.homebuilt not
   in .newsrc--subscribe? [ynYN]
   ```

2. Press **y** or **n** to indicate whether you want to subscribe.
3. If you do, the program then asks *where* in the list of newsgroups you'd like to see this one, like this:

   ```
   Put newsgroup where? [$^L]
   ```

4. Press **$** to put the newsgroup at the end of your list of newsgroups. Press + followed by the name of an existing group to put it after that group.

News Netiquette

Respectful, civilized Net communication and behavior.

The list of mail etiquette rules listed in Part 2 apply equally to news articles if not more so because *far* more people read news articles than read a piece of e-mail. Here are some other rules:

- Don't post a follow-up to the whole group that is intended solely for the author of the original article.

- Be sure each article is appropriate for the group to which you post it.
- Don't post a two-line follow-up that quotes an entire 100-line article. Edit down the quoted material.
- Most groups make available a periodic Frequently Asked Questions (or *FAQ*) message that answers many questions you might ask. Check for a FAQ message before asking a question.

If you have access to FTP, all FAQ messages are available on the system `rtfm.mit.edu`.

Newsgroups

Groups of Usenet messages filed by topic.

Usenet newsgroups have multipart names separated by dots, such as `comp.dcom.fax` (a group about fax machines and fax modems). When a bunch of groups are related, they have related names. For example, all the groups having to do with data communication are filed under `comp.dcom`.

The Usenet newsgroup hierarchy is listed in the following table:

Name	Description
`comp`	Topics having something to do with computers. Lots of fairly meaty discussions.
`sci`	Topics having something to do with one of the sciences, also fairly meaty.
`rec`	Recreational groups about sports, hobbies, the arts, and other fun endeavors.
`soc`	Social groups, both social interests and plain socializing.
`news`	Topics having to do with net news itself. A few groups with general announcements, otherwise not very interesting unless you're a news weenie.
`misc`	Miscellaneous topics that don't fit anywhere else. (The ultimate miscellaneous group is called `misc.misc`).
`talk`	Long arguments, frequently political. Widely considered totally uninteresting except to the participants.
`alt`	Unofficial "alternate" newsgroups, ranging from the topical to the weird to the totally stupid.

Regional and organizational hierarchies also exist. For example, the `ne` hierarchy is for topics of interest to New England, ny for New York, `ba` for the San Francisco Bay Area, and so forth.

Universities and other organizations big enough to have their own net news communities often have hierarchies of their own, like `mit` for M.I.T.

Each system manager can decide which newsgroups to receive and which to skip. Due to the volume, almost nobody gets them all. On a UNIX system, you can see the list of newsgroups that are available on your system by looking at the file `/usr/lib/news/active`.

See *The Internet For Dummies*, Chapter 11, section "The newsgroup thicket" and Chapter 12 for more detailed lists of network newsgroups and hierarchies.

The Order of Newsgroups

3

The sequence of newsgroups as they appear on your news reader.

You can control the order in which trn presents groups. If you tell it to present the most interesting ones first, you can move quickly through your favorite groups by pressing spacebar or **n**. The first group that you usually see is called `general` and is supposed to be articles of general interest on your machine.

In practice, the newsgroup `general` tends to fill up with junk, and you should move it toward the end of your list of groups.

The following describes how to control the order of your newsgroups:

1. Press **m** (for move).
2. If you want to move the current group, press Enter. To move some other group, type the group's name followed by Enter.
3. To move the group to the end of the list so that it's the last one you see, press **$**.
4. To move the group to the beginning of the list so that it's the first one you see, press ^ (a caret, usually Shift-6).
5. To move the group to appear after another group, press +, then type the name of the other group, and then press Enter.

To see a list of all the groups you subscribe to (or have ever subscribed to) press **L** (uppercase). To see a list of groups you *don't* subscribe to, press **l** (lowercase).

Reading Messages in a Newsgroup

Reading the actual *news.*

When you enter a newsgroup (by pressing spacebar when `trn` asks whether you want to read the messages in the group), `trn` shows you the first screen of the first unread message or *article* in the group. You can read each article that you haven't read yet, skip over articles that look boring, reply to messages, print them, or save them.

A group of messages on a single topic is called a *thread.* If a topic looks boring, you can tell `trn` to skip entire threads.

Press spacebar when `trn` or `rn` suggests a group to indicate that you want to read the group. (See "Reading the News" in this Part.)

To read the messages in a newsgroup, press spacebar when `trn` asks whether you want to read them.

You see the first message that you have not yet read, something like

```
general #6281      (1)
From: root-Admin(0000)     (1)
[1] Disk space     (1)
Organization: I.E.C.C.     (1)
Date: Sat Aug  7 06:48:03 1993     (1)
+                           [1]
The disks are nearly full again. Please delete
unneeded files, or we'll delete some for you.
(Yes, that's a threat.)
--
Your friendly system manager
End of article 6281 (of 6282)—what next? [npq]
```

More info

The first line of the article in the preceding screen example tells you the name of the newsgroup (`general`) and the message number within the group (`6281`). The last line tells you how many articles are in the newsgroup (`6282`) and which one you are looking at again (`6281`, which means that there is one more unread message in this newsgroup). It also asks what you want to do next.

Your choices are the following:

- If the message is too long to fit on the screen, press spacebar to see the next screen (much like `more` and `pg` UNIX commands).
- If you're done looking at this article, press **n** to go on to the next one.
- If you are done reading articles in this newsgroup, press **q** to go on to the next group.
- If you don't feel like reading any of the unread articles in the newsgroup, press **c** to "catch up" — that is, *pretend* that you've read all of the articles.

Once you get the hang of it, you'll mostly press spacebar to go to the next article or newsgroup, **n** to skip an article or newsgroup, and **k** to skip a group of articles (described in next section). Until you prune the set of newsgroups you're subscribed to down to something reasonable, you'll probably also be hitting **u** frequently to get rid of the large majority of groups that you don't want to read.

3

Keystrokes for reading articles

Key	Meaning
Spacebar	Read the next page of the current article, or the next unread article.
n	Skip to the next article.
k	Kill this article and any others with the same title.
K	Same as *k,* but also enter the title in the kill file so the title is *rekilled* each time you enter the group.
q	Leave this group.
c	Catch up (pretend you've read all articles in this group).
u	Unsubscribe to this newsgroup.
s*file*	Save article to a file named *file.*
|lpr	Feed article to command *lpr* (this is the easiest way to print an article).
/*xyz*	Find the next article whose title contains *xyz.*
=	Show titles of unread articles.
Ctrl-L	Redraw the screen.
Ctrl-R	Restart the current article (redisplays the first page).
X	Unscramble *rot13* message (not for the squeamish).

Key	Meaning
e	Extract uudecoded or shar file (see "Extracting Binary Files" in this Part).
edir	Extract into directory *dir*.
h	Show extremely concise help.
q	Leave this group.

Reading the News

Using a news reader to read net news.

Several programs help you read the news. The most widely used are `rn` and its variant `trn`. Most other programs are similar, although details differ.

In nearly all news-reading programs, you don't need to press Enter (or Return) after single-letter commands. However, some commands require that you type a line of text *after* the letter, such as a filename or a newsgroup name. In that case, you do press Enter to indicate that you're done with the line of text.

1. Run the `trn` program.
2. If the system says that it's not found, run `rn` instead.

   The first time you run the program, it does some automatic setup, as in the following:

   ```
   % trn
   Trying to set up a .newsrc file—running newsetup...
   Creating .newsrc in /usr/johnl to be used by news
   programs.
   Done. If you have never used the news system before,
   you may find the articles
   in news.announce.newusers to be helpful.  There is
   also a manual entry for rn.
   To get rid of newsgroups you aren't interested in,
   use the 'u' command.
   Type h for help at any time while running rn.
   Unread news in general     14 articles
   (Revising soft pointers—be patient.)
   Unread news in ne.food     47 articles
   Unread news in ne.forsale 1177 articles
   ```

```
Unread news in ne.general 268 articles
Unread news in ne.housing 248 articles
etc. ********  14 unread articles in general—read
now? [+ynq]
```

Your news reader now suggests a newsgroup for you to read.

More info

`trn` (or `rn`) keeps a list of the newsgroups that you are interested in — that is, those that you are *subscribed to*. If you are not interested in a newsgroup, you can *unsubscribe*. When new newsgroups are created, `trn` asks whether you want to subscribe to them.

To start off, `trn` assumes that you are subscribed to all newsgroups, and you must unsubscribe to those you don't care about. After the very first time you run `trn`, you don't see the first few lines of the preceding screen example — you just see the list of newsgroups to which you are subscribed and the number of unread messages in each of them. If you are subscribed to a whole bunch of newsgroups (more than about five), it only lists the first few.

Keystrokes for selecting newsgroups

The following table contains a list of keystrokes that you use when selecting newsgroups:

Key	Meaning
Spacebar or y	Enter the next group that has unread news (see "Reading Messages in a Newsgroup" in this Part).
n	Skip this group for now (see "Skipping over Newsgroups" in this Part).
u	Unsubscribe from this group so that you don't see it anymore (see "Unsubscribing to Newsgroups").
g	Go to a group; type the group name after the g (see "Finding a Newsgroup" in this Part).
q	Quit, leave `trn` or `rn`.
p	Go to the previous group with unread news.
h	Show extremely concise help.
Ctrl-L	Redraw the screen.

See *The Internet For Dummies*, Chapter 11, section "Hand-to-Hand Combat with News."

Replying to and Following Up Articles

Means just what it says.

You can respond to an article in two ways:

- You can send e-mail to the article's author, known as a *reply*.
- You can write an article of your own to the network at large, known as *posting a follow-up article*.

Sending an e-mail reply

1. While reading the original article, press **r** (lowercase). If you want to include some or all of the text of the article in your reply, press **R** (uppercase) instead.

   `trn` or `rn` starts a text editor (usually `vi` or `emacs`), with a skeleton of the reply message already provided. If you pressed **R**, it includes a copy of the original article.

2. Type in your reply. If you started with the original article, edit out the irrelevant parts.
3. Save the file and leave the editor.

   `trn` or `rn` asks if you want to send, abort, or edit the response. To send the message, press **s**. If you changed your mind, press **a** to abort the reply, sending nothing.

   It asks if it should add your standard signature (stored in your file `.signature`). Press **y** unless you already signed the article.

Posting a news followup

1. While reading the original article, press **f** (lowercase) to send a follow-up. If you want to include some or all of the text of the article in your followup, press **F** (uppercase) instead.
2. It asks if you're sure you want to send a followup to the whole Net. If you're sure that's what you want to do, press **y**.

   `trn` or `rn` starts a text editor, with a skeleton of the follow-up message already provided. If you pressed **F**, it includes a copy of the original article.

3. Type in your follow-up. If you started with the original article, edit out the irrelevant parts.

4. Save the file and leave the editor.

   It asks whether to send the followup. Press **y** to send it, or **a** to abort and not send it.

All news articles that you send, including follow-ups, automatically add your `.signature` file. So don't put in the signature yourself, or it'll appear twice.

Saving Articles

Saving news articles in files (just like e-mail messages).

To save an article you are reading, press **s** followed by the name of the file in which to save it. If the file doesn't already exist, `trn` or `rn` asks whether it should make the file a mailbox. Press **y**. If you save multiple articles in a mailbox-format file, you can use any of the mail programs discussed in Part 2 to handle the file.

If you don't specify a directory, articles are saved in files or mailboxes in your directory `News`. You can put articles in other directories by specifying the directory name, but `News` is usually as good a place as any.

See *The Internet For Dummies*, Chapter 11, section "Just a few notes for our files."

Selecting the Threads You Want to Read (trn Only)

Means just what it says.

After you tell `trn` or `rn` to enter a newsgroup, there may be so many articles that even killing and junking them *still* leaves too many to read. Instead, you can select only those subjects that you *do* want to see.

`trn` has a feature called *thread selection* that makes the selection easy, but `rn` doesn't have this feature.

Sample

1. Enter the desired newsgroup by pressing + or spacebar (rather than `y`).

You see a screen like this:

```
general                   14 articles

a 0000-uucp(0000)         3  New mail paths
b 0000-Admin(0000)        10  backup

d Chet Arthur             1  System will be down
                          to clean hampster cages

-- Select threads -- All [Z>] --
```

The preceding screen example is a "table of contents" for the newsgroup. The first line tells you the newsgroup name and the number of articles. The subsequent lines list the threads, with a one-letter identifier (for example, `d`), the author of the first article in the thread (`Chet Arthur`), the number of messages in the thread (1), and the subject (`System will be down to clean hampster cages`). The last line asks which thread you want to read.

2. Select the threads you want by pressing the appropriate letters (the one-letter identifers). To select a range of threads, press the letter of the first one, followed by a hyphen, and then the letter of the last thread.
3. To go to the next page of threads, press right-arrow.
4. To start reading the threads you've selected, press **Z** or Tab.

If you want to read all of the threads on the current screen, simply press **Z** or Tab without selecting any of them.

To junk (arrange to never see) the threads that aren't selected, press **D**. The most effective way to pick just the articles of interest is to select the interesting threads on each screen, using the key letters, and then press **D** to quickly skip the rest of the threads on that screen.

The spacebar is set up to pick the command you are most likely to want at the end of each screen. If there is another screen of threads, pressing spacebar does the same thing as right-arrow (goes to the next screen). On the last screen, spacebar is the same as **Z** (to start reading articles).

Keystrokes for thread selection

The following table lists key letters that are useful in thread selection:

Key	Meaning
Spacebar	Read the next page of the table of contents or start reading selected articles if no more threads in the table of contents

D	Start reading selected articles, mark unselected articles as read
Z	Read selected articles
/*xyz*	Select articles whose titles contain *xyz*
d-g	Select articles `d` through `g` in the current table of contents
c	Catch up by pretending you've read every article in the group (recent versions of `trn` only)
h	Show extremely concise help
q	Leave this group

Sending New Articles

3

Post a brand-new article to a newsgroup.

You can start your own thread by posting an article.

Just make sure

- Your article is on an interesting topic.
- The newsgroup didn't just discuss it at length last week.
- You have your facts straight.

Here's how to do it:

1. Within `trn` or `rn`, enter the newsgroup of interest.
2. If you're in the thread-selection screen, press > to get to the article-reading screen (`trn` only).
3. Press **j** to tell it you're not reading any article.
4. Press **f** (as though you were writing a follow-up article to something).
5. It asks if you're sure you want to write an article. If you are, press **y**.
6. When you are prompted to do so, enter a new subject for the article.
7. Write the new article the same way you'd write a follow-up (described in the previous section).

If you're not running `rn` or `trn` at the moment, you can use the `Pnews` command to post news directly. At the command prompt, type **Pnews** followed by the name of the newsgroup to post to. Then follow the preceding directions for posting an article.

Some newsgroups are *moderated.* This means that articles are not posted directly as news. Instead, articles are e-mailed to a human moderator, who actually posts the article if it's appropriate to the group. Moderators, being human, do not process items instantaneously, so it can take a day or two for items to be processed. If you write an article for a moderated group, the news-posting software tells you that it is mailing your item to the moderator.

See *The Internet For Dummies*, Chapter 11, section "So You Want to Be Famous?"

Skipping Over Newsgroups

Bypassing a newsgroup.

When `trn` asks whether you want to read a newsgroup now, you can skip over it just this once but remain subscribed to the newsgroup. To skip a group for now, press **n** to say no, don't read it now.

Unsubscribing to Newsgroups

Making a newsgroup go away.

When `trn` asks whether you want to read a newsgroup, you can *unsubscribe* — that is, tell it that you never want to hear about the newsgroup again. To unsubscribe from a group, press **u**, and you will not see the group at all in the future.

Part 4

On-Line Communication

Several facilities can put you into direct contact with other computers on the Internet:

- finger checks the status of a computer or person.
- rlogin lets you log into other computers on the Net as though you were connected to them directly (see also telnet).
- rsh is a junior version of rlogin.
- talk and ntalk let you chat with, or type back and forth to, someone else on another computer.
- telnet and tn3270 let you log into other computers on the Net as though you were connected to them directly (see also rlogin).

There are many on-line ways to find public systems to which you can telnet or rlogin.

- Scott Yanoff publishes a regularly updated on-line resource guide. finger yanoff@csd4.csd.uwm.edu to find out how to get a copy.
- The Washington University Libraries in St. Louis, Missouri offer WorldWindow, a gateway to dozens of login services. telnet to library.wustl.edu (no login needed).
- hytelnet is a system that provides access to libraries around the world. You can access catalogs, on-line books, and other information. telnet to access.usask.ca, info.ccit.arizona.edu, nctuccca.edu.tw, info.mcc.ac.uk, or rsl.ox.ac.uk, and log in as hytelnet. Or telnet to laguna.epcc.edu or info.anu.edu.au and log in as library.

finger

Checks the status of a computer or person.

finger — Checking Up on Other Computers

Displaying the status of other computers on the Net.

On line-oriented systems, type **finger@** (that's an *at* sign) followed by the host computer's name on the command line, like this:

```
finger @shamu.ntw.org
```

On windowing systems, start `finger` and then enter the machine name into the appropriate field in the program window.

`finger` returns a list of the people currently using the remote computer. The format varies considerably from one system to another, but the following is a typical list:

```
Login   Name            TTY  Idle  When       Office
root    0000-Admin      co    12:  Wed 16:04
johnl   John R. Levine  vt     1d  Wed 16:03  Rm 201A
johnl   John R. Levine  p0         Wed 16:10  Rm 201A
johnl   John R. Levine  p1      1  Wed 16:10  Rm 201A
```

finger — Checking Up on Other People

Displaying the status of people using other computers on the Net.

On line-oriented systems, type **finger** followed by the user's name, then @ (that's an *at* sign) followed by the host computer's name on the command line, as in

```
finger johnl@iecc.com
```

On windowing systems, start `finger` and then enter the user and machine names into the appropriate fields in the program window.

The result varies from machine to machine. The following is typical:

```
Login name: johnl        In real life: John R. Levine
Directory: /usr/johnl   Shell: /bin/sh
On since Jun 30 16:03:13 on vt01    9 hours Idle Time
Project: Working on "Internet for Dummies Quick Ref"
Plan: Write many books, become famous.
```

On many systems, you can have information displayed when someone *fingers* you. You can put a one-line summary in the file `.project` and a longer description (up to ten lines or so) in `.plan`.

Many organizations, particularly universities, let you use `finger` to look up information like phone numbers and office locations. For example, to find someone at the Massachusetts Institute of Technology, enter

`finger` ***`lastname-firstname`*** **`@mit.edu`**

Similar servers exist at Yale (`@directory.yale.edu`), Boston University (`@bu.edu`), the University of California at San Diego (`@ucsd.edu`), and other schools. A few companies also have directory servers. You can always try to access such a server — the worst that can happen is you won't get a useful answer back.

finger — *Getting Other Information*

Means just what it says.

Some systems use `finger` as an easy way to query databases. The available information ranges from the profound to the silly. For example,

- `Finger nasanews@space.mit.edu` for a list of recent NASA press releases.
- `Finger copi@oddjob.uchicago.edu` for an almanac of today's birthdays, anniversaries, and sports events.
- `Finger quake@geophys.washington.edu` for a list of earthquakes in the past few days.
- `Finger nichol@stavanger.sgp.slb.com` for a list of regularly posted Usenet FAQs (frequently asked questions) and other informative messages.
- `Finger info@drink.csh.rit.edu` or `coke@cs.cmu.edu` for the current status of some on-line Coke machines.

These `finger` commands frequently return more than one screenful of stuff. On windowing systems, you can scroll the answer in the `finger` program's window. But on line-oriented systems, the response flies off the top of the screen. If you're using a UNIX workstation, use the `more` command to see the result a page at a time, like this:

```
finger someservice@somesite | more
```

See *The Internet For Dummies*, Chapter 9, sections "They won't mind if you give them the finger," "Fingering far-off friends for fun," and "The industrial-strength finger."

rlogin

Lets you log into other computers on the Net as though you were connected to them directly.

rlogin — *Connecting to Remote Computers*

Accessing other computers as if you were using one of their terminals.

`rlogin` can automatically take care of logging you into the other system.

If `rlogin` doesn't work, use `telnet` instead. `rlogin` is considerably less widely supported than `telnet`.

1. Type **rlogin**, followed by a space, and then the name of the computer:

   ```
   rlogin shamu
   ```

2. After `rlogin` connects to the remote computer, everything you type is sent to the remote computer, and its responses are returned to your screen. You are usually logged in automatically.

If your username on the other computer is different from your username on your own computer, type **-l** and then the username, as in

```
rlogin shamu -l king
```

To arrange for an automatic login, see "`rlogin`—Logging In Automatically" elsewhere in this Part.

`rlogin` may ask what kind of terminal you're using (common terminal types include VT100, ANSI, and 3101). If `rlogin` suggests a terminal type, accept it and see what happens.

See *The Internet For Dummies*, Chapter 14, section "Remote Login: The Next Best Thing to Being There."

`rlogin` — Disconnecting from Remote Computers

Ending an `rlogin` session.

The normal way to disconnect from a remote computer is to log out from the remote computer, usually by typing **logout** or **exit**.

If the other end doesn't let go, press Enter, followed by **~.** (tilde, period), and then Enter again. `rlogin` ends the connection and exits.

`rlogin` — Logging In Automatically

Arranging for `rlogin` and `rsh` (see following section) to log you in without asking for your name or password.

If a group of computers is administered together, it is often set up as a shared user community — that is, anyone allowed to log into one computer can log into all. In this case, someone creates a system file that lists all the hosts whose users are *equivalent*, or who have access to all the computers. This system file is called `/etc/hosts.equiv` on UNIX systems (and something similar on other machines).

For example, if machine `able` has a `hosts.equiv` file that contains the name of machine `baker`, anyone on `baker` can `rlogin` to `able` by using the same username and without giving a password.

If your computer group uses the NIS (Sun's Network Information System, previously known as Yellow Pages), which shares ID information among a group of computers, the system consults an NIS `hosts.equiv` database as well as its regular `hosts.equiv` file. To see the database, type **ypcat hosts.equiv**.

If you hold accounts on several hosts that are *not* all under the same management, you must arrange your own `rlogin` setup:

1. Create a file called `.rhosts` on each UNIX machine (called `rhosts` on other machines).

2. In the file `.rhosts`, list all the other host computers on which you have accounts. Type the host name, followed by a space, and then type your username.

   For example, if your username is *sam* on systems `able` and `baker`, and *tilden* on system `clarissa`, your `.rhosts` files should contain

   ```
   able sam
   baker sam
   clarissa tilden
   ```

3. Try using `rlogin` to connect to another host computer. The system you're logging into checks your `.rhosts` file and sees whether you're listed.

See *The Internet For Dummies*, Chapter 14, sections "Be My Guest" and "Be My Host."

rsh

A junior version of `rlogin`; runs only one command at a time on a remote system.

(For information regarding an automatic login, see the section "`rlogin` — Logging In Automatically" elsewhere in this Part.)

1. Run `rsh`, entering the name of the remote system and the command to run, as in the following:

   ```
   rsh shamu who
   ```

   The preceding command runs the `who` command on a computer named `shamu`.

2. If your login name on the other system is different from the one you use on your own computer, include it on the command line after typing **-l**:

   ```
   rsh shamu -l king who
   ```

On some UNIX systems, `rsh` runs a useless *restricted shell*. In such cases, this command's name is `remsh` or `rshell` instead of `rsh`.

`rsh` doesn't properly run full-screen programs that take character-at-a-time user input, such as text editors like `emacs` or `vi` or mail programs like `elm` or `pine`. To run these programs, use `rlogin` instead.

See *The Internet For Dummies*, Chapter 14, section "How to Hardly Be There at All."

talk

Lets you chat with, or type back and forth to, someone else on another computer.

The talk commands split the screen in half: what you type appears in the top half, and what the other person types appears in the bottom half.

Some systems have "old talk" called talk and "new talk" called ntalk. If your system has both, use ntalk.

talk — *Ending a* talk *Session*

"Hanging up" when you're done with your talk session.

Either party can end the talk session. To end it, press your *interrupt key* (usually Ctrl-C or Del). talk displays [Connection closed. Exiting] and breaks the connection.

talk — *If You Don't Want to* talk

Declining to engage in a talk session.

You can choose not to talk.

- To turn off talk requests, type **mesg n** at the command prompt.
- To turn on talk requests, type **mesg y** at the command prompt.
- To find out whether you're receiving requests, type **mesg** at the command prompt.

If you try to talk to someone who has turned off talk requests, talk displays [Your party is refusing messages]. Likewise, if others try to talk to you, and you have turned off talk requests, they'll see that same message.

Some commands turn off talk requests while they run (they simply want to keep the screen clear). Therefore, if your request to talk is refused, try again a few minutes later. Your request may have been blocked by a program protecting its screens rather than denied by someone who's not feeling chatty.

See *The Internet For Dummies*, Chapter 13, section "Talking the Talk."

talk — Responding to Someone Else's Request to talk

"Answering" someone who is requesting to `talk` to you.

1. When someone else wants to `talk` to you, your computer displays something like this:

   ```
   Message from Talk_Daemon@shamu ...
   talk: connection requested by king@NTW.ORG.
   talk: respond with:  talk king@NTW.ORG.
   ```

2. If you want to `talk`, type the command that `talk` suggests (in this case, type **talk king@NTW.ORG**).
3. `talk` splits the screen and reports `[Connection established]`.
4. Start typing.

talk — Starting a Conversation

Initiating a `talk` session.

1. Type **talk**, followed by the user's name, @ (at sign), and finally the host computer's name.

   In other words, you usually can type

   talk *mail address*

2. `talk` notifies the other person and displays `[Waiting for your party to respond]` on your screen.
3. When the other person responds, `talk` displays `[Connection established]`, at which point you can start typing.

telnet

Enables you to log into other computers on the Net as if you were connected to them directly.

Don't worry — it's perfectly legal!

telnet — Connecting to Remote Computers

Accessing other computers as if you were using one of their terminals.

1. Type telnet followed by the host name of the computer you want to log into. On line-oriented systems, you type the host name on the command line. On windowing systems, you type the host name into a pop-up window.
2. telnet connects your computer to the remote system.

   Note: In the process of connecting, telnet tells you the *escape character*, which is the key combination that you should press if you have trouble disconnecting from the remote computer.
3. Log into the remote system as though you were directly connected. Usually, it asks you to enter your username on that system and then your password. Some systems don't need a login and move directly to a welcome screen.

After telnet makes contact with the remote computer, it may ask you what kind of terminal you're using (common terminal types include VT100, ANSI, and 3101). If you indicate the wrong type, the information on your screen will be scrambled. If telnet suggests a terminal type, accept it and see what happens.

4

Connecting to IBM mainframes

Many IBM mainframe computers expect you to use a terminal known as a 3270. The regular telnet program, however, is lousy at pretending to be a 3270. So, if you're talking to an IBM mainframe, try using tn3270 rather than telnet; you get snappier responses and better-looking screens.

In addition, unlike regular telnet, tn3270 lets you use cursor keys reliably to move anywhere on-screen. This innocuous-sounding feature is important because IBM 3270 terminals typically display screens full of blank fields. When you finish filling in the blanks, you press Enter to send everything to the remote computer. Regular telnet, however, expects you to type a line at a time. Worse, in full-screen programs, the remote system must update the screen after every keystroke.

If you're not sure whether you've contacted an IBM mainframe computer, remember that IBM mainframes use LOTS OF CAPITAL LETTERS and acronyms such as VM, CMS, and MVS.

Using nonstandard port numbers

Most systems provide `telnet` access on the standard `telnet` port — port number 23. A few systems, though, use a different port to provide direct access to a particular service. In these cases, you must know the port number to use.

- On line-oriented systems, type the port number after the system name on the command line.

  For example, `telnet martini.eecs.umich.edu 3000` is a system that looks up place names in the U.S.

- On windowing systems, type the port number where you select the system you want to connect to.

You disconnect and exit the same way you do for a normal `telnet` connection, by logging out from the remote system, or by pressing the escape character (usually Ctrl-]) — see "`telnet` — Disconnecting from Remote Computers" elsewhere in this Part.

See *The Internet For Dummies*, Chapter 14, section "How You Can Be in Two Places at Once."

telnet — *Disconnecting from Remote Computers*

Ending a `telnet` session by logging out and ending the connection.

Log out from the remote system as if you were connected directly. `telnet` closes the connection and (on most systems) exits. Usually, you log out by typing **logout** or **exit** or **bye**.

On windowing systems, if `telnet` doesn't exit, use the standard technique to close a window. For example, in Microsoft Windows, double-click the box at the window's upper left-hand corner.

If the remote system is recalcitrant and doesn't log you out, try the following steps. On line-oriented systems:

1. Type the escape character, which is usually Ctrl-] (close square bracket). You should see a prompt like

   ```
   telnet>
   ```

   If you don't get the `telnet` prompt in a second or two, press Enter.

2. Type **quit** and press Enter.

   `telnet` closes the connection and exits.

On windowing systems, simply choose from the menu the item that disconnects the remote system.

Part 5

Moving Files

The Internet allows you to copy files between your computer and other computers on the Net. The standard facilities are known as

- FTP (*File Transfer Protocol*)
- RCP (*Remote Copy*)

If your system doesn't handle FTP or RCP directly but does have e-mail, you may be able to use e-mail to retrieve files from the Internet. See the section "FTP — FTP Via Mail Servers" in this Part.

FTP

Internet facility that enables you to copy files between other computers and your computer.

FTP — Connecting to a Remote System

Logging onto a computer on the Net for purposes of copying files to or from your computer.

Most FTP programs accept commands that you type. A few of them — particularly under Microsoft Windows — use a fancier screen interface. See the section "FTP — Full-Screen FTP Programs" elsewhere in this Part.

1. Run the `ftp` program by typing **ftp** followed by the name of the system to connect to:

```
ftp ntw.org
```

2. You see a message confirming that you are connected. Then the program asks for a login name and password. If you have an account on that system, use the same name and password that you use for a direct or `telnet` login, as in the following:

```
Connected to shamu.ntw.org.
220 iecc FTP server (Version 4.1 8/1/91) ready.
Name: elvis
331 Password required for elvis.
Password: type password here
```

More info

On most systems you can create a file called `.netrc` (or plain `netrc` on non-UNIX systems) that contains the login name to use on each system that you use often. Each line lists a machine, the login name, and the password for that machine, like this:

```
machine shamu.ntw.org login elvis password sinatra
```

When you `ftp` to the preceding system, it logs you in automatically.

On some versions of FTP, you can place a default line at the end of the `.netrc` file that says what login name to use for systems that are *not* listed, as in the following:

```
default login anonymous password elvis@ntw.org
```

See *The Internet For Dummies*, Chapter 16, section "What's On File?"

FTP — Anonymous FTP

Connecting to Internet systems that provide files available to the public.

On systems that provide files for public download, rather than logging in with your own name, you log in as `anonymous` and use your e-mail address — or the word `guest` — as the password.

Sample

1. Run the `ftp` program by typing **ftp**.
2. When the remote computer asks for your login name, type **anonymous**.
3. When the remote computer prompts for your password,

enter your e-mail address. If the system suggests guest as the password, type **guest** instead.

```
ftp internic.net
Connected to internic.net.
220 *****Welcome to the InterNIC Registration Host *****
Name: anonymous
331 Guest login ok, send "guest" as password.
Password: type e-mail address or guest here
230 Guest login ok, access restrictions apply.
```

See *The Internet For Dummies*, Chapter 16, section "No Names, Please."

FTP — Downloading to Your PC

Retrieving files to your PC from your dial-up Internet host.

If you are using a local PC to dial into an Internet host, FTP retrieves files to the Internet host, *not* to your local PC. After the files are on your Internet host, you still have to download them to get them to your PC.

Downloading details vary but generally resemble the following:

1. Type the command to the host to start the downloading program, such as **sz** for Zmodem or **kermit** for Kermit, followed by the names of the files to download.
2. If your PC terminal program doesn't start downloading automatically, tell it to start downloading (typically with an Alt-key combination — refer to your terminal program's manual).
3. After the files are downloaded, delete the copies on the Internet host so that you aren't charged for the disk space.

The Terminal program that comes with Microsoft Windows 3.1 can transfer binary files using either Xmodem or Kermit. To choose a protocol, use the Settings ➪ Binary Transfers command. To begin a file transfer, use the Transfers ➪ Receive Binary File command.

See *The Internet For Dummies*, Chapter 16, section "The File-Retrieval Roundup."

FTP — FTP Via Mail Servers

Retrieving files from remote computers, using e-mail to gain access to FTP.

If your system supports e-mail but not FTP, you can still get limited access to FTP by using a *mail server*, a system that receives e-mail messages and mails back files. Many systems that support anonymous FTP also have mail servers.

For example, `rtfm.mit.edu`, the system that archives all of the periodic Usenet information messages for FTP, also has a mail server with the address `mail-server@rtfm.mit.edu`.

To find out how to use a mail server, mail it a message containing the line:

```
help
```

Mail servers vary a lot from system to system, but they all can send you a help message. To use the server, you typically send it commands like the following:

```
index
send somefile from somegroup
```

In the preceding screen example, the first command sends an index, and the second retrieves a particular file.

See *The Internet For Dummies*, Chapter 17, section "Waaah! I Can't FTP."

FTP — Full-Screen FTP Programs

Connecting and copying files from a Windows or Macintosh machine using a full-screen FTP program.

Many Mac and Windows FTP programs use a full-screen interface like the figure on the next page.

- To connect to a remote system, select the Connect item from the menu. (Once connected, the item usually changes to a Disconnect item, as in the figure.)
- To change to a different local or remote directory, click the mouse on the desired directory and then click on the appropriate Change arrow.
- To copy a file, click on the file to copy and then click on the appropriate Copy arrow.
- To switch between ASCII (text file) and Binary (non-text file) copying, click on the appropriate button.

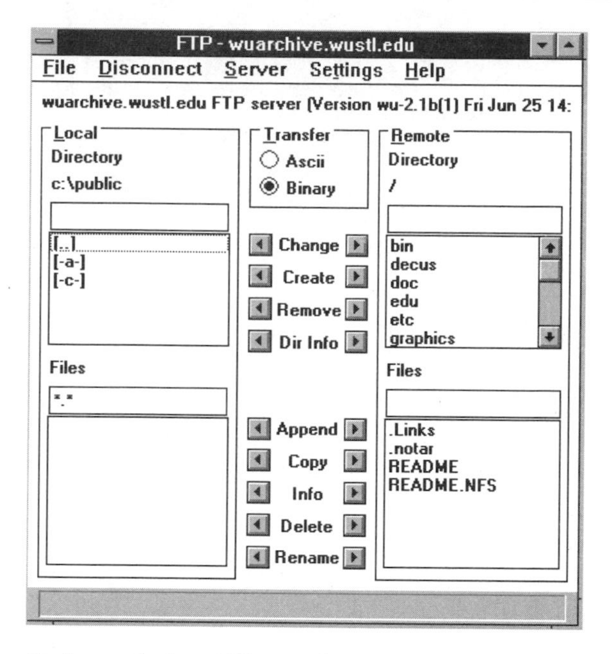

Underneath the spiffy, windowed program, FTP is actually running the same commands as the conventional `ftp` program. Windowed FTP programs can take a while to start up because they run `dir` commands to get the file lists for the selection windows.

See *The Internet For Dummies*, Chapter 16, section "Once again, PCs don't leave well enough alone."

FTP — Generic FTP by Mail Servers

Retrieving files by mail using systems that FTP the files for you.

If all else fails, a few systems will FTP files for you from any public source. Typically, you send the system a list of the commands that you *would* have typed to FTP, as in the following:

```
FTP ftp.internic.net
USER anonymous
cd fyi
get fyi-index.txt
quit
```

To find out exactly how to use a generic FTP server, send it a `help` message to start. You can use the following list of public FTP-by-mail servers — just remember to send your request to the server that is closest to you:

E-mail address	*Location*
`ftpmail@decwrl.dec.com`	California
`bitftp@pucc.princeton.edu`	New Jersey
`bitftp@vm.gmd.de`	Germany
`ftpmail@ftp.uni-stuttgart.de`	Germany
`ftpmail@grasp.insa-lyon.fr`	France
`bitftp@plearn.edu.pl`	Poland
`ftpmail@doc.ic.ak.uk`	England

More info

The FTP-by-mail system is very, very popular, and each server has a daily limit of the number of files it will retrieve. This means that it may take as long as a week to answer your request. Don't send it again; that won't help.

See *The Internet For Dummies*, Chapter 17, section "WAAHHH! I Can't FTP!"

FTP — Leaving FTP

Disconnecting from the remote computer after copying files.

Type **quit**, and FTP exits, as follows:

```
ftp> quit
221 Goodbye.
```

If you use a fancy Microsoft Windows or Macintosh program, see the section "FTP — Full-Screen FTP Programs" earlier in this Part.

FTP — Listing the Files in Directories

Looking for the files you want to retrieve after you log in.

Sample

Type **dir** (for *directory*). You see lots of messages, including a list of the files and subdirectories in the current directory. It looks something like this:

```
ftp> dir
200 PORT command successful.
150 Opening ASCII mode data connection for /bin/ls.
total 23
drwxrwxr-x 19 root      archive   512 Jun 24 12:09 doc
drwxrwxr-x 5 root       archive   512 May 18 08:14 edu
drwxr-xr-x 31 root      wheel     512 Jul 12 10:37
systems
drwxr-xr-x 3 root        archive  512 Jun 25
1992 vendorware
 ... lots of other stuff ...
226 Transfer complete.
1341 bytes received in 0.77 seconds (1.7 Kbytes/s)
```

More info

If the directory is so big that it doesn't fit on the screen, you can ask for just part of it using *wildcards*. For example, typing **dir c*** asks for just the files starting with the letter *c*.

If you want to store the directory listing on your own computer, you can enter the name of a local file that you want to store the listing in. Use the `dir` command followed by a . (*dot*, to indicate that you want a listing of the current directory), followed by the filename in which to store the result, like this:

```
ftp> dir . file-list
200 PORT command successful.
150 Opening ASCII mode data connection for /bin/ls.
226 Transfer complete.
45341 bytes received in 42 seconds (1.0 Kbytes/s)
```

5

FTP — Moving to Other Directories

Nosing around the remote computer looking for files.

1. Type **cd** followed by the name of the directory you want to change to, like this:

```
ftp> cd edu
250 CWD command successful.
```

2. Then type the **dir** command to see what's in the new directory.

On many systems, all the interesting stuff is stored in a directory called `pub`.

See *The Internet For Dummies*, Chapter 16, section "The Directory Thicket."

FTP — Retrieving Files

Copying files from the remote computer to your own computer.

First, you set up to retrieve the files, and then you retrieve them using the `get` command.

Sample

1. Use the `cd` command to move to the directory on the remote computer that contains the file(s) you want.
2. If the files are not plain text, type **image** to tell FTP to transfer the files as binary images, not text files, as in the following:

```
ftp> image
200 Type set to I.
```

3. Type **get**, followed by the filename on the remote computer, and then the filename to use on your computer (the local filename), as shown in the following. (If you want to use the same name, you can omit the local filename.)

```
ftp> get intro.txt info-file
local: info-file remote: intro.txt
200 PORT command successful.
150 Opening ASCII mode data connection for
intro.txt (5243 bytes).
226 Transfer complete.
5359 bytes received in 0 seconds (5.2 Kbytes/s)
```

4. FTP retrieves the file and displays a message about it.

More info

It can take FTP a long time to retrieve a large file. For a file retrieved from a distant site, you should allow one second for every 1,000 characters in the file.

If you retrieve a non-text file, and it arrives smashed and unusable, 95 percent of the time the problem is that you forgot to type **image** before you retrieved it. If you realize part-way through retrieving a file that you forgot to type **image** first, you can interrupt it by typing your interrupt character — usually Ctrl-C or Del. In windowing systems, click on Cancel. Interrupting the retrieval process can take 30 seconds or so.

See *The Internet For Dummies*, Chapter 17.

FTP — Retrieving Groups of Files Using mget

Copying a group of files with one `mget` command.

1. Move to the directory that contains the files and, if appropriate, set image mode by typing **image** (see the section "FTP — Retrieving Files" in this Part).
2. Type **mget** (for *Multiple Get*) followed by the names of the files you want to get. You can also use filename patterns that match multiple filenames. The most commonly used pattern is * which means all files in the directory.
3. mget asks you about each file that matches the names and patterns in the list. Press **y** to transfer the file, **n** to skip it.

Use the `prompt` command to turn off the prompting for each file so that it transfers all the files in the group without asking.

FTP — Storing Files on Remote Systems

If the permissions set on the remote system allow, you can store files to the remote system as well.

Sample

1. Type **cd** followed by the directory name on the remote computer to move to the directory into which you want to store the file.

2. If the files contain binary data, set image mode (as described in the topic "FTP — Retrieving Files").
3. Type **put**, followed by the filename on your computer (the local filename), followed by the filename to use on the remote system. (You can omit the remote filename if it's the same as the local filename.) See the following example:

```
ftp> put nigel nigel-data
local: myfile remote: stored-file
200 PORT command successful.
150 Opening ASCII mode data connection for nigel-
data.
226 Transfer complete.
795 bytes sent in 0 seconds (0.78 Kbytes/s)
```

More info

You can copy a group of files to the remote computer using the `mput` command (which stands for *Multiple Put*). Follow the steps in the preceding example except in step 3 type **mput**, followed by the name of the files to store or a pattern that matches the name of the files to store. The pattern * means all files in the local directory.

As it copies the files, `mput` asks you about each file. Type **y** to store it, **n** to skip it.

To store a group of files without FTP asking you about each one, type **prompt** to turn off name prompting.

See *The Internet For Dummies*, Chapter 16, section "About, Face!"

FTP — Summary of FTP Commands

A short list of useful FTP commands.

A few of the commands in the following table are not otherwise mentioned in this book:

Command	Description
`get` *old new*	Copy remote file *old* to local file *new*. You can omit *new* if same name as *old*.
`put` *old new*	Copy local file *old* to remote file *new*. You can omit *new* if same name as *old*.
`del` *xyz*	Delete file *xyz* on remote system.

cd *newdir*	Change to directory *newdir* on the remote machine.
cdup	Change to next higher directory (the parent directory).
lcd *newdir*	Change to directory *newdir* on the local machine.
asc	Transfer files in ASCII mode (use for text files).
bin	Transfer files in binary or image mode (all other files).
quit	Leave ftp.
dir *pat*	List files whose names match pattern *pat*. If you omit *pat*, list all files.
mget *pat*	Get files whose names match pattern *pat*.
mput *pat*	Put files whose names match pattern *pat*.
mdel *pat*	Delete remote files whose names match pattern *pat*.

See *The Internet For Dummies*, Chapter 16, section "An FTP Cheat Sheet."

FTP — Uncompressing and Decoding Retrieved Files

Means just what it says.

Files on anonymous FTP systems are usually stored *compressed* — that is, in one of several forms that save space and make them easier to transfer but require that you decode them. Often they are *archived* as well, with a group of files stored as one file. And some files are pictures or images that require particular programs to display them. The filename extension (the part after the dot) tells you how the file is coded and (more importantly) which program to use to decode it.

5

Many compression and uncompression programs can be FTPed from wuarchive.wustl.edu in the directory /packages /compression.

There are far too many ways to store data in files. The following table lists the main categories of files found on FTP servers.

Type	Description
Archived	Many files combined into one (most archived files are also compressed)
Compressed	A coded form that saves space, with many variants

Type	*Description*
Images	Digitized pictures in GIF, JPEG, or other image format
Text	Plain text that can be printed, displayed, and edited with the usual printing and text-editing programs
Uuencoded	Special format that disguises a non-text file as text so it can be e-mailed

See *The Internet For Dummies*, Chapter 17, section "How Many Kinds of Files Are There?"

cpio

Files with the extension `cpio` (lowercase) are the products of `cpio` (CoPy In and Out), a UNIX program with its own format.

To decode ("uncpio") the file `blurfle.cpio` on a UNIX system, type **cpio -itcv < blurfle.cpio**.

Compressed `cpio` is also common. Uncompress the file and then uncpio.

See *The Internet For Dummies*, Chapter 17, section "In the Archives."

GIF

CompuServe GIF (Graphics Interchange Format) is a popular image format. Most image display programs display `GIF` files directly.

gz *and* z

Files with the extensions `gz` and `z` (lowercase) are created by the GNU `gzip` program. They are uncompressed by GNU `gunzip`.

`gzip` and `gunzip` are available at `ftp.uu.net`, `prep.ai.mit.edu`, and other places.

GNU `gunzip` knows about a lot of compression formats and can decompress most compressed formats that aren't also archive formats.

See *The Internet For Dummies*, Chapter 17, section "Packing It In."

JPEG

JPEG (Joint Photographic Experts Group) is a popular compressed image format. Most image display programs display JPEG files directly. JPEG images often have the extensions `.JPG` or `.JIF`.

See *The Internet For Dummies*, Chapter 17, section "For the Artistically Inclined."

tar

Files with the extension `tar` (lowercase) are the products of `tar` (Tape ARchive), a UNIX archiving program. On a UNIX system, to unpack a `tar` file, type **tar xvf blurfle.tar**.

`tar` files commonly are also compressed and have names like `blurfle.tar.Z`. Uncompress them and then untar. On some systems, these are called `TAZ` files.

Z

Files with the extension `Z` (uppercase) are compressed files created by the UNIX `compress` program. They are decoded with the program `uncompress`.

ZIP

Files with the extension `ZIP` are *compressed archives* created by the shareware PKZIP program or free ZIP utilities, and can be *unpacked* with the shareware program PKUNZIP or the free program UNZIP, both widely available.

These compression programs are available on `ftp.uu.net` in `/pub/zip`.

RCP

A somewhat easier facility than FTP, used to transfer files on systems that support it.

5

RCP — Copying All the Files in a Directory

Using the `rcp` program to copy multiple files in a directory to or from a remote computer.

To copy all the files from the current directory on the remote computer to the current directory on your computer, type **rcp**, followed by the remote directory name, then **.** (dot, which stands for the current directory), and finally the **-r** (for *recursive*) flag, as in the following:

```
rcp pumpkin:projectdir .
```

The preceding line says to copy the directory `projectdir` on host `pumpkin` into the current directory (indicated by a period) on the local machine.

To copy all the files from the current directory on your local computer to the current directory on the remote computer, type **rcp,** followed by **.** (dot, which stands for the current directory), then the remote directory name, and finally the **-r** (for *recursive*) flag.

See *The Internet For Dummies*, Chapter 16, section "A Few Words from Berkeley."

RCP — Copying Files from Remote Computers

Using the rcp program to copy files from remote computers to your computer.

The rcp command is available on the same computers that support rlogin and rsh — that is, mainly UNIX systems (see the sections on rlogin in Part 4 of this book).

Type **rcp**, followed by the remote filename, followed by the local filename.

For example, to copy a file named mydata from the host named pumpkin to the local machine and call it pumpkindata, type the following:

```
rcp pumpkin:mydata pumpkindata
```

rcp doesn't say a thing if the file transfers successfully. If a problem occurs, it displays a message.

More info

To use the rcp command, the remote system must be set up so that it can log you in automatically to do the copy. See the sections on rlogin in Part 4 of this book.

In RCP, you refer to a file on another system with the system's hostname, a colon, and the filename — for example, othersys:myfile. If the file is in another directory, use the usual slash separator, as in othersys:dirname/myfile.

To copy a file if your username is different on the other system, just type your username followed by @ (*at* sign) before the host name, as in the following:

```
rcp steph@pumpkin:mydata pumpkindata
```

To copy to or from another user's directory on the remote computer — and if the permissions allow this — use ~ (tilde) followed by the username as the directory name:

```
rcp pumpkin:~tracy/somefile tracyfile
```

`rcp` is extremely taciturn and says nothing at all unless something goes wrong. If you are copying a lot of files over a network, it can take a while (like a couple of minutes), so you may have to be more patient than usual while waiting for it to do its work.

If you get tired of waiting and want to stop RCP, type the interrupt character, usually Ctrl-C or Del.

See *The Internet For Dummies*, Chapter 16, section "A Few Words from Berkeley."

RCP — Copying Files to Remote Computers

Uploading a file to a remote computer that supports `rcp`.

Type **rcp**, followed by the local filename, followed by the remote filename. For example, to copy a file named `pumpkindata` from the local computer to the host named `pumpkin` and call it `mydata`, type the following:

```
rcp pumpkindata pumpkin:mydata
```

`rcp` doesn't say a thing if the file transfers successfully. If a problem occurs, it displays a message.

Part 6

Finding Resources

So many resources are available on the Internet that finding them can be harder than using them. In this Part, you'll find ways to look for resources.

Much of this Part deals with the various aspects of using Archie, a very handy system that keeps enormous lists of files and helps you find anonymous FTP files on the Internet.

Gopher and the World Wide Web, two facilities described in Part 7, are excellent ways to look for resources.

Archie

An Internet facility that scans Archie servers to find available files, using criteria that you provide.

Archie — Finding Public Archie Servers

Listing some public Archie servers that you may use.

All the servers in the following lists have the same data available. Therefore, you should choose one close to you.

U.S. public Archie servers

Name	Location
archie.sura.net	Maryland
archie.unl.edu	Nebraska
archie.rutgers.edu	New Jersey
archie.internic.net	New Jersey
archie.ans.net	New York

International public Archie servers

Name	Location
archie.au	Australia
archie.edvz.uni-linz.ac.at	Austria
archie.univie.ac.at	Austria
archie.uqam.ca	Canada
archie.funet.fi	Finland
archie.th-darmstadt.de	Germany
archie.ac.il	Israel
archie.unipi.it	Italy
archie.kuis.kyoto-u.ac.jp	Japan
archie.wide.ad.jp	Japan
archie.hana.nm.kr	Korea
archie.sogang.ac.kr	Korea
archie.nz	New Zealand
archie.inesc.pt	Portugal
archie.rediris.es	Spain
archie.luth.se	Sweden
archie.switch.ch	Switzerland
archie.ncu.edu.tw	Taiwan
archie.doc.ic.ac.uk	United Kingdom
archie.hensa.ac.uk	United Kingdom

Archie — Requesting Information from Archie

Means just what it says.

Archie search modes

Archie has four different search modes. How much you know about the name of the file(s) you're looking for determines the search method that you should use. The four different search modes along with their meanings follow:

Method	Meaning
sub	Match the search string anywhere in the filename, disregarding capitalization. (This is the mode it uses by default.)
subcase	Match the search string exactly as given anywhere in the filename, including matching capitalization.
exact	Search for this exact filename, including matching capitalization. Use this option if possible — it's the fastest.
regex	Use UNIX *regular expressions* to define the pattern for Archie's search. (See the next section for more information.)

Special characters in Archie regular expressions

The following is a list of special characters to use in Archie regular expressions, along with what they mean:

Character	Meaning
*	Matches any number of whatever it follows
[*xyz*]	Match any one of the characters in the brackets
^	Matches the beginning of the name. Inside square brackets, it means to match any character except the ones in the brackets
$	Matches the end of the name

For example, `^[0-9]*$` matches a name consisting entirely of digits, and `tr.ck` matches *trick, track, truck,* or *trzck*.

See *The Internet For Dummies*, Chapter 19, section "Searching is such sweet sorrow, or something."

6

Archie — E-Mail to Archie

Using e-mail to communicate with an Archie server.

You can submit Archie queries by e-mail:

1. Send an e-mail message to `archie@`*server*, where *server* is any of the Archie servers listed in the section "Archie — Finding Public Archie Servers," earlier in this Part.
2. The contents of the message are commands in nearly the same form as you give to `telnet` Archie. (See the upcoming table of Archie commands in this section.)
3. Archie mails back its response.

The following table lists e-mail Archie commands:

Command	*Description*
`prog`	Searches assuming a regular expression search (regex)
`whatis`	Supply the keyword for the software description database search
`compress`	Send the reply in a compressed and uuencoded format
`servers`	Returns a list of Archie servers
`path`	Gives the e-mail address you want Archie to use to respond to your mail request, in case the return address in your mail isn't correct
`help`	Return the help text for e-mail Archie
`quit`	Ends the request to Archie

The most common commands are `prog` and `whatis`. For example, typing the following command searches for files with filenames that start with `font` and end with `.txt`:

```
prog font.*txt
```

Archie servers are so heavily loaded that it can take several minutes for a `telnet`, command line, or window Archie command to run. In that case, you may as well mail your request so you don't have to wait while it thinks. Also, for large queries, a 400-line e-mail message is usually easier to handle than a 400-line `telnet` or windowed response.

See *The Internet For Dummies*, Chapter 19, section "E-Mail archie."

Archie — `telnet` to Archie

The usual way of using Archie.

Unless you have a local Archie program, you usually `telnet` to Archie. Here's how to do it:

1. `telnet` to the nearest Archie site (see the section "Archie — Finding Public Archie Servers" elsewhere in this Part).

   See Part 4 to learn how to use the `telnet` command.

2. Log in as `archie`, no matter who you actually are.

   It responds with an `archie>` prompt.

3. If you don't want to use the standard sub search (described in the section "Archie — Requesting Information from Archie," elsewhere in this Part), type

   `set search` ***`xxx`***

   where the ***xxx*** is the type of search you want (**sub, subcase**, **exact**, or **regex**).

4. Type **prog** followed by the string to search for.

   Archie returns a list of the matching files.

5. To get a description of a name or term, type **whatis** followed by the name or term.

6. After making as many searches as you want, type **exit** to exit.

7. Use anonymous FTP (see Part 5) to retrieve the files.

See *The Internet For Dummies*, Chapter 19, section "Telnet Archie"

Archie — Using the `archie` Program

Using the `archie` program if you have it on your computer.

If your system has an `archie` program, you can make Archie queries directly:

1. Type **archie** followed by the string to search for, as in

   ```
   archie prune
   ```

   Archie returns a list of the matching files, with directory and host names.

2. Use anonymous FTP (see Part 5) to retrieve the files.

Archie usually returns more than one screenful of answers. To view the list one page at a time, use the | character and the `more` command, as in

```
archie garlic | more
```

To save the list in a file, use the > character to redirect the list, like this:

```
archie garlic > garlicfiles
```

You can use the following options to control how the `archie` program works.

Archie Modifier	*Equivalent Telnet Command*	*Meaning*
`-c`	`subcase`	Set search mode for a case-sensitive substring
`-e`	`exact`	Set search mode for an exact string match (default)
`-r`	`regex`	Set search mode for a regular expression search
`-s`	`sub`	Set search mode for a substring search
`-l`		List one match per line
`-t`	`sortby`	Sort the output by date, newest first
`-m#`	`maxhits`	Set the maximum number of matches to return (default 95)
`-h` *host*		Specify the Archie server to use
`-L`		List the known Archie servers and the current default

See *The Internet For Dummies*, Chapter 19, section "Straight Archie."

Archie — Ways of Using Archie

Different methods of using Archie to help find files available for anonymous FTP.

For more information on FTP (File Transfer Protocol), see Part 5 of this book.

All Archie does is accept a keyword or pattern that you enter and look it up in the database of FTP files that are kept on an Archie server.

You can use Archie in the following ways — each of them requires that you contact an Archie server:

- Command-line archie program
- E-mail to an Archie server
- Telnet to an Archie server
- Windowed xarchie program

Finding Mailing Lists

Means just what it says.

SRI International maintains a "list of lists," a lengthy list of Internet mailing lists:

- You can FTP it from sri.com, from the directory netinfo, with the filename interest-groups (plain text) or interest-group.Z (compressed).
- You can get it by e-mail; for details send a message consisting of the single word *help* to mail-server@sri.com.

Stephanie da Silva maintains the Usenet listing of publicly accessible mailing lists, probably the most up-to-date and complete listing available (see Part 3 of this book for more on Usenet). Here are three ways to get it:

- It's available posted monthly to the Usenet groups news.lists, news.announce.newusers, and news.answers.
- It's available via FTP from the Usenet archive at rtfm.mit.edu. Go to the directory /pub/usenet /news.answers/mail/mailing-lists and get files part1 through part8. (By the time you read this there may be more than eight parts!)
- It's available via e-mail from mail-server@rtfm.mit.edu. Send a message consisting of the single word *help* to get started.

Usenet Archive at rtfm.mit.edu

Obtaining the Usenet archive at rtfm.mit.edu.

The Usenet archive at `rtfm.mit.edu` is a treasure trove of useful information and references to archives elsewhere on the Net (see Part 3 of this book for more on Usenet). The archive is indexed by the names of Usenet groups. There are two easy ways to get it:

- The archive is available via e-mail from `mail-server@rtfm.mit.edu`. Send a message consisting of the single word *help* to get started.
- `ftp` to `rtfm.mit.edu`, change directory to `usenet-by-groups`, and then go to the newsgroup you are interested in — for example, `sci.med` for information about medicine.

(See Part 5 of this book for information about FTP.)

xarchie — *Using* xarchie

A windowed version of `archie` available on windowed UNIX systems.

Users of the X Window System and its relatives such as Motif can use `xarchie`:

1. Run `xarchie`.

   It displays a window like the one in the following figure.

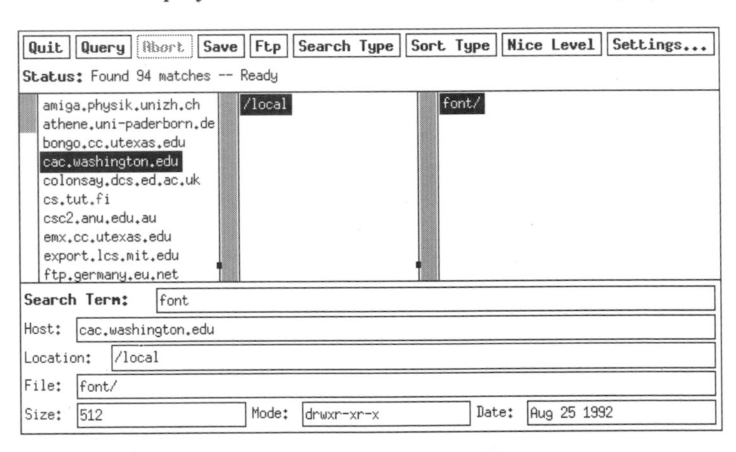

2. If the standard sub search mode isn't satisfactory, click on Search Type and select the desired type from the menu.
3. Move the cursor to the Search Term: box and type the search string there.
4. Click on Query to perform the search.

   `xarchie` displays the results in three columns.

5. To see the files and directories found in a system name in the first column, click on the system name.

   `xarchie` displays the names in the second column.

6. To see the files and subdirectories found in a directory name in the second column, click on the directory name.

See *The Internet For Dummies*, Chapter 19, section "Xarchie."

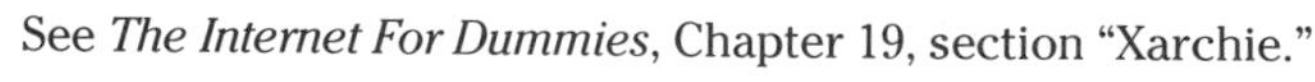

xarchie — *Retrieving Files*

Means just what it says.

Unlike other versions of Archie, `xarchie` can retrieve the files whose names it's found:

1. Normally, files are retrieved to the current directory. To use another directory besides the current one, select Settings... to get the settings window, shown in the following figure:

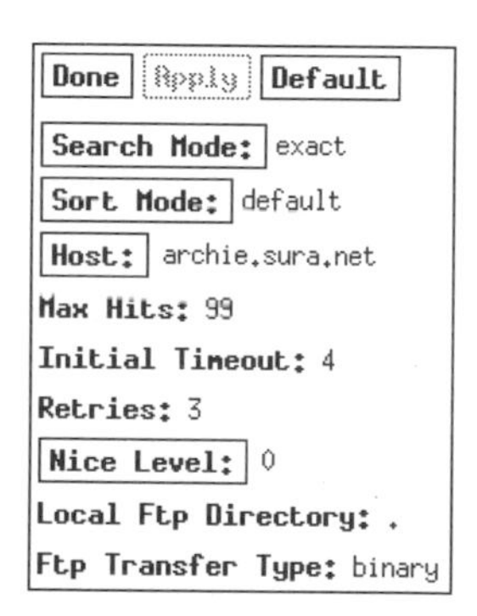

2. Move the cursor to Local Ftp Directory setting and type the directory name. Click on Done.

3. To retrieve the displayed file(s), click on FTP.

   `xarchie` retrieves the file(s).

See *The Internet For Dummies*, Chapter 19, section "Xarchie."

Part 7

Interactive Information Facilities

Gopher, WAIS (Wide Area Information Service), and WWW (World Wide Web) are new Internet facilities that make it easier to find and retrieve network information. Their functions overlap, but all three have significantly different strengths.

- Gopher is the easiest to use because it presents you with lots of simple menus. It's the easiest for finding files and interactive services.
- WAIS is harder to use but can do full-text searches in a tremendous number of databases. It's the best to use to search for information that hasn't already been indexed for Gopher or WWW.
- WWW presents information in a friendly hypertext format, although not as many WWW databases exist as do Gopher or WAIS databases. If the material that you want has been set up in WWW, it's by far the most fun to use.

If you're looking for a particular file or piece of information, like a copy of *The Wonderful Wizard of Oz* or the current weather in Key West, Gopher is the quickest way to find it. If your goal is something obscure, WAIS is your best bet because — unlike the other two — WAIS doesn't depend on someone already having indexed the information. If you just want to browse in a general topic area, WWW is the quickest way to have a look around.

If you know the filename that contains the information you want, you can use Archie, which is described in Part 6 of this book.

Gopher

An Internet search system that lets you navigate through "Gopherspace," presenting information as a series of menus.

The menus can be physically distributed all over the world and can include documents, images, and other sorts of data. Gopher provides a way to find files on systems all over the Net, including information that comes from the `finger` program, Archie, `telnet`, FTP, and so forth.

Gopher — Finding Gopher Programs

Locating a Gopher program to use so that you can utilize Gopher servers.

Ideally, there would be a Gopher program (known in tech-speak as a *Gopher client*) such as the original UNIX `gopher`, `xgopher`, or `gopherbook` on your machine. Such Gopher programs connect to *Gopher servers*, which are the machines out there on the Internet that actually provide the information.

If your system doesn't have a Gopher program, you can `telnet` directly to one of the public Gopher servers listed in the following tables, all of which run the original UNIX `gopher` program. Use the login name listed in the table if you want to use Gopher. If no login name is listed, log in as **gopher**.

U.S. public Gopher servers

Name	Location	Login
infoslug.ucsc.edu	California	
infopath.ucsd.edu	California	infopath
grits.valdosta.peachnet.edu	Georgia	
uxl.cso.uiuc.edu	Illinois	
gopher.netsys.com	Illinois	enews
panda.uiowa.edu	Iowa	
inform.umd.edu	Maryland	
seymour.md.gov	Maryland	
gopher.ora.com	Massachusetts	
wsuaix.csc.wsu.edu	Michigan	wsuinfo

consultant.micro.umn.edu	Minnesota	
gopher.msu.edu	Mississippi	
nicol.jvnc.net	New Jersey	NICOL
sunsite.unc.edu	North Carolina	
twosocks.ces.ncsu.edu	North Carolina	
cat.ohiolink.edu	Ohio	
envirolink.hss.cmu.edu	Pennsylvania	envirolink
ecosys.drdr.virginia.edu	Virginia	
gopher.virginia.edu	Virginia	gwis
telnet.wiscinfo.wisc.edu	Wisconsin	wiscinfo

International public Gopher servers

Name	*Location*	*Login*
info.anu.edu.au	Australia	info
finfo.tu-graz.ac.at	Austria	info
nstn.ns.ca	Canada	fred
camsrv.camosun.bc.ca	Canada	
tolten.puc.cl	Chile	
gopher.denet.dk	Denmark	
ecnet.ec	Ecuador	
gopher.th-darmstadt.de	Germany	
gopher.isnet.is	Iceland	
siam.mi.cnr.it	Italy	
gopher.torun.edu.pl	Poland	
gopher.uv.es	Spain	
info.sunet.se	Sweden	
gopher.chalmers.se	Sweden	
hugin.ub2.lu.se	Sweden	
gopher.brad.ac.uk	United Kingdom	info

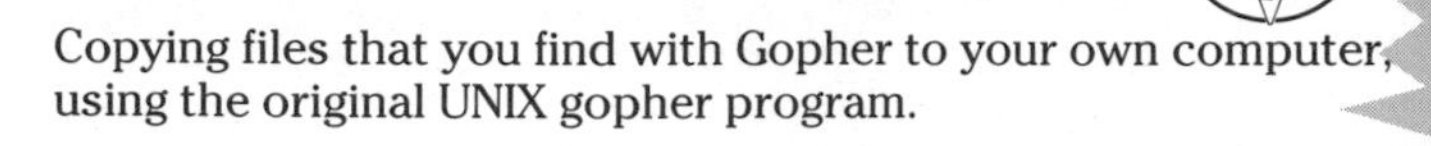

Gopher — Saving Files

Copying files that you find with Gopher to your own computer, using the original UNIX gopher program.

Note: This works only if you are using a Gopher client program on your own computer, not if you `telnet` to a Gopher server.

- For text files, `gopher` shows the file a screen at a time. Press the spacebar to move from screen to screen or press **q** to stop viewing the file.
- Press **s** to save the file on your own computer.
- Press **m** to send the file to you as e-mail. It asks for your e-mail address.

(See Part 2 of this book for information about e-mail.)

Downloading using PC terminal programs

If you dial into a UNIX `gopher` program from a PC using a terminal program such as Kermit, Crosstalk, or Procomm, you can download files directly to your system.

1. On the menu in which the file appears, move the cursor to the file item but do not press Enter.
2. Press **D** (for Download).

   `gopher` pops up a window listing the download schemes that it can use, with numbers by each one.
3. Type the number of a download scheme that your terminal program supports, most often Kermit, Zmodem, or Xmodem.
4. If it doesn't do so automatically, tell your modem program to start downloading. The information is copied to your disk.

Gopher — Searching with gopher

Telling the UNIX `gopher` program to search its database based on text you enter.

If you can't find the information you're looking for by moving around the menus (as described in the section "Gopher — Starting `gopher`," elsewhere in this Part), try *searching.*

In `gopher` menus, menu items that can be searched are indicated by <?>.

1. Run `gopher` as described in the section "Gopher — Starting `gopher`," elsewhere in this Part.
2. Select a search item by moving to it and pressing Enter.

3. gopher pops up a box into which you can type search terms. Type a word or a few words that describe what you are looking for and press Enter.

   gopher shows you a menu consisting of the items that matched.

4. Select items on that menu as you would on any other menu.

More info

gopher has special *CSO* searches for looking up people in organization phone books. They work nearly the same way as regular searches, except that you can type in lots of different facts about the person you're looking for. Generally, just type the person's first name followed by last name and press Enter. That's usually enough to find someone.

A program called Veronica searches through all available Gopher menus to find items that match your words. It's a quick way to find something whose name you know. To find a Veronica search item, look on the Home Gopher menu, which is usually available on the first menu gopher shows you.

Gopher — Starting gopher

Running the gopher program on a UNIX system to see Gopher information.

1. If you use a UNIX system that has the gopher program, skip to the next step. Otherwise, use the telnet program to log into a UNIX system that has gopher.

   See Part 4 of this book for how to telnet.

2. Run the program by typing **gopher**.

   You'll see a menu like this:

```
Internet Gopher Information Client v1.1
Root gopher server: gopher.micro.umn.edu

→ 1. Information About Gopher/
  2. Computer Information/
  3. Discussion Groups/
  4. Fun & Games/
  5. Internet file server (ftp) sites/
  6. Libraries/
  7. News/
```

```
 8. Other Gopher and Information Servers/
 9. Phone Books/
10. Search Gopher Titles at the University
    of Minnesota <?>
11. Search lots of places at the University
    of Minnesota <?>
12. University of Minnesota Campus Information/

Press ? for Help, q to Quit,u to go up a menu
Page: 1/1
```

3. To move to a particular item, use the up- and down-arrow keys or type the line number of the item. Items that end with a slash display other menus, items that end with something in <> are search or `telnet` items (discussed elsewhere in this Part of the book), and items that end with neither are files.

   To select an item, move the cursor to it and press Enter.

4. To exit Gopher, press **q**. If it asks if you really want to quit, press **y**.

If the menu is larger than the screen, press + and - (or use the arrow keys) to scroll it up and down. To return to the previous menu, press **u**. To return to the first menu, press **m**.

Gopher — Summary of Commands

Listing some commands used by the UNIX `gopher` program.

The following table contains basic UNIX `gopher` commands:

Command	Meaning
`Enter`	Select current item, same as cursor right
`u`	Up, go back to previous menu, same as cursor left
`+`	Move to next menu page
`-`	Move to previous menu page
`m`	Go to main menu
digit(s)	Go to particular menu item, terminate with Enter
`/`	Search menu for string
`n`	Search for next match
`q`	Quit, leave `gopher`
`=`	Describe current item

The following table contains UNIX gopher bookmark commands:

Command	Meaning
a	Add current item to bookmark list
A	Add current menu to list
v	View bookmarks as a menu
d	Delete current bookmark

The following table contains UNIX gopher file commands:

Command	Meaning
m	Mail current file to user
s	Save current file (not for telnet)
p	Print current file (not for telnet)
D	Download current file

Gopher — Using Bookmarks in gopher

Telling gopher to place *bookmarks* at particular menus and items for later reference.

You can use bookmarks to remember interesting places as you navigate through Gopherspace.

- To put a bookmark on the current item, press **a** (lowercase).
- To put a bookmark on the current menu, press **A** (uppercase).
- To see a menu of all of your bookmarks, press **v**.
- To select an item from that menu, move the cursor to it and press Enter.
- To delete an item from the bookmark menu, move the cursor to it and press **d**.

More info

If you telnet to gopher, bookmarks are only remembered until you log out. If you run gopher on your local computer, bookmarks are remembered in a file and are available any time.

Gopher — Using gopher to telnet

Using the gopher program to telnet to another system.

If you find something interesting in gopher, and gopher says that you have to telnet to another system to see it, Gopher offers to do the telnetting for you automatically. On Gopher menus, telnet items end with <TEL>.

(See Part 4 of this book for information on telnet.)

1. Select a telnet item by moving the cursor to it and pressing Enter.

   gopher pops up a window that warns you that you are about to telnet to someplace else and gives you the login name to use.

2. The telnet session starts. Log in when prompted to, using the name supplied.
3. Use the system to find the information you wanted.
4. When you log out, you return to gopher.

More info

Any system that gopher can telnet to, you can telnet to yourself. If you find a telnetted system useful, make a note of the name of the system and the login name and then telnet there directly next time.

See *The Internet For Dummies*, Chapter 20, section "Leaping Tall Systems in a Single Bound" and sidebar "How Many Telnets Would a Telnet Telnet if a Telnet ..."

Gopher — Using Gopher's Menus

Means just what it says.

All Gopher programs have one feature in common — they show you a series of menus. Gopher menus can contain the following types of items:

- Menu items referring to other menus
- File items referring to files of text, images, or other data
- Search items that let you type in some search text and create a custom menu of items found in the search
- telnet items that start an interactive telnet session to a host which provides a particular service. If you need to login to the host, Gopher tells you the login to use.

The content of each menu is determined by the remote Gopher server, not the Gopher client program. Therefore, no matter which program you use, you can get to the same material. Some Gopher client programs have limits on the kinds of files they can handle; in particular, the UNIX `gopher` program can only display files that contain plain text, although it can copy any file to your local machine if you want to deal with it later.

See *The Internet For Dummies*, Chapter 20, sections "Welcome to Gopher," "The Good, the Bad, and the Ugly," and "Where Do I Find a Gopher?"

Using HGOPHER under MS Windows

A graphical user interface for Gopher that runs under Microsoft Windows.

Its operations are generally similar to those of `xgopher`. To start it, follow these steps:

1. In Program Manager, double-click on the HGOPHER icon.

   HGOPHER displays a screen like this:

   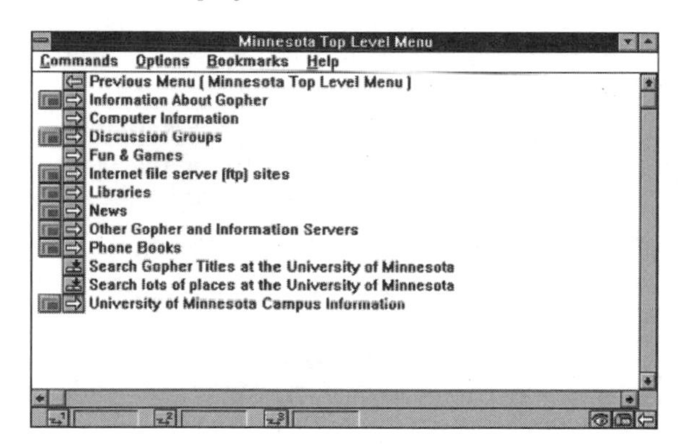

   The column of icons describe the file type. The eyeglasses mean a text file, arrows are menus, the little arrow pointing at the book is a search item. The 1101 is a binary file. `telnet` items (none shown here) appear as little terminals.

2. To select an item, click on its icon. If there is a second icon to the left of the item, click on that icon to find out some extra information describing the item.

   When you select a search item, HGOPHER pops up a window into which you type search terms. When you select a file item, HGOPHER starts up a suitable program to view that item (such as Windows Notepad for a text file).

If you click on the eyeball at the lower right-hand corner of the screen, when you select a file item, HGOPHER asks you for a local filename into which to copy the file, allowing you to save files locally. Click on the eye again to return to viewing selected files.

When you select a `telnet` item, HGOPHER pops up a window telling you the login name to use. When you click on OK, it opens a `telnet` window to the remote system.

HGOPHER can have up to three file and `telnet` windows open at one time, and you can continue moving through menus while it is retrieving a file to be displayed.

See *The Internet For Dummies*, Chapter 20, section "High-Class Gopher."

xgopher — *Saving/Printing Files*

Printing files or saving files to your computer after the `xgopher` program finds them.

If you select a file item, `xgopher` opens a window viewing that file. You can then save or print the file by following these steps:

- To scroll the file up and down, click on Page Down and Page Up menu buttons or click in the scroll bar at the left side of the window.
- To save the file, click on Save To File, move the mouse pointer to the filename box in the Save to file window, type the filename to use, and click on OK.
- To print the file, click on Print.
- To end viewing the file and close the file's window, click on Done.

You can leave file windows open and return to the main `xgopher` window. This lets you open several file windows at once. If several windows are open, move the mouse pointer to the window that you want to work with.

xgopher — *Searching*

Telling `xgopher` to search for items, based on text that you enter.

If you can't find the information you are looking for by moving around the menus, try searching. In `xgopher`, menu items that can be searched are indicated by `<idx>`.

1. Select the item by double-clicking on it.
2. When xgopher opens the Index Search window, move the insertion point to the empty box in that window and type in one or more search terms.
3. Click on Do Index.

   xgopher performs the search, and creates a menu of items that satisfied the search.

xgopher — *Starting the program*

Starting the graphical user interface for Gopher.

If you are using the X Window system or one of its relatives such as Motif, you can use xgopher.

(If you use Microsoft Windows on a PC, see the section "Using HGOPHER under MS Windows" earlier in this Part.)

1. To start xgopher, type **xgopher** in a shell window or select it from a menu if one is available.
2. To select an item on a menu, click on it with the mouse and then click on the Fetch Selection menu button or just double-click on the item.
3. To leave xgopher, click on Quit.

If an xgopher menu doesn't fit in the window, click the left or right mouse button in the gray scroll bar at the left of the window to scroll it up or down.

xgopher — *Using Bookmarks*

Telling xgopher to place *bookmarks* at particular menus and items for later reference.

You can use bookmarks to remember interesting places as you navigate through Gopherspace.

- To put a bookmark on an item, click on the item and then click on Add Selection as Bookmark.
- To put a bookmark on the current menu, click in a blank area of the xgopher window and then click on Add Directory as Bookmark.

The current bookmarks are displayed in a menu in the lower part of the xgopher window. To select a bookmark, double-click on its item in the lower window. To delete a bookmark, click once on its entry in the lower window and then click on Remove Bookmark.

xgopher — Using xgopher to telnet

Means just what it says.

If you find something interesting in xgopher and it says that you have to telnet to another system to see it, xgopher offers to do the telnetting for you automatically. On xgopher menus, telnet items end with <tel>.

1. When you click on a <tel> item, xgopher telnets to a remote system for you.
2. xgopher may first display a window telling you the password to use. Click on OK.
3. A window opens for the telnet session. Log in with the password provided.
4. Use the system to find the information you wanted.

   (See Part 4 for how to telnet.)
5. When you log out from the remote system, the telnet window closes.

TIP

You can continue using xgopher while the telnet window is open — just move the mouse pointer back to the xgopher window. You can even have several telnet windows open at once to different hosts.

WAIS

Wide Area Information Service, an Internet full-text search facility.

WAIS —Searching for Text

A full text search service.

You give WAIS a list of words, and it looks through a big set of documents and finds the ones that best match the search words. Unlike Archie (see Part 6), WAIS looks at the *contents* of files, not just at the titles of files.

Some versions of WAIS also feature *relevance feedback.* After WAIS does a search, you can mark a few of the documents that it found as most relevant and then redo the search, in which case it tries to find more documents similar to the ones that you marked.

1. If your computer system has a WAIS program, run it.

2. If not, `telnet` to a computer that has WAIS (see Part 4 of this book for more on `telnet`). We recommend telnetting to `quake.think.com`, the home of WAIS. Log in as **wais**.
3. WAIS starts out showing a single entry, the *directory of servers* (also known as *sources*).
4. Use WAIS to search for information (see other WAIS entries in this Part of this book).
5. When you are done, escape from WAIS by pressing **q**.

   Depending on where you are, you may have to press it three or four times to get out of the program.

More info

There are three basic steps in any WAIS search:

1. Decide which document sources to search.
2. Enter search words and do the search.
3. Retrieve interesting documents and possibly do a revised search.

See *The Internet For Dummies*, Chapter 21, "We Have WAIS of Finding Your Information."

WAIS — Searching for Text in Documents

Telling WAIS what words or phrases to search for.

Note: Before you can search for text within documents, be sure that you have already selected the document sources to search in.

1. After you have selected the WAIS document sources you want, press Enter to prepare to search.
2. WAIS shows you the current list of keywords. You can press Ctrl-U to clear it if need be and then add new terms if desired.

3. Press Enter again to perform the search. The result resembles the following figure:

```
SWAIS                              Search Results                              Items: 40
  #     Score      Source                      Title                              Lines
001:   [1000] (cmns-moon.think)  SUMMER-PUDDING(D)               USENET Cookbook    59
002:   [1000] (        recipes)  Anne Louis Re: BREAD: Bread Recipes Coll         1101
003:   [ 826] (cmns-moon.think)  XMAS-PUDDING(D)                 USENET Cookbook   107
004:   [ 780] (cmns-moon.think)  WIGILIA-1(M)                    USENET Cookbook   110
005:   [ 570] (cmns-moon.think)  YOGURT-FROZ-1(D)                USENET Cookbook    56
006:   [ 559] (cmns-moon.think)  FRUIT-TART(D)                   USENET Cookbook    51
007:   [ 547] (cmns-moon.think)  FRUIT-CAKE-1(C)                 USENET Cookbook   104
008:   [ 547] (cmns-moon.think)  CURRIED-FRUIT(D)                USENET Cookbook    59
009:   [ 535] (cmns-moon.think)  FRUIT-SOUP(SPV)                 USENET Cookbook   110
010:   [ 524] (cmns-moon.think)  FRUIT-SALAD(D)                  USENET Cookbook    97
011:   [ 524] (cmns-moon.think)  BRAN MUFFINS 2(D)               USENET Cookbook    64
012:   [ 524] (cmns-moon.think)  AMBROSIA(D)                     USENET Cookbook    46
013:   [ 512] (cmns-moon.think)  CHOC PUDDING 2(D)               USENET Cookbook    08
014:   [ 512] (cmns-moon.think)  BREAKFAST CAS(M)                USENET Cookbook    73
015:   [ 512] (cmns-moon.think)  BREAD-STUFF-1(S)                USENET Cookbook    71
016:   [ 500] (cmns-moon.think)  TRIFLE-1(D)                     USENET Cookbook    64
017:   [ 500] (cmns-moon.think)  SODA-BREAD(B)                   USENET Cookbook    79
018:   [ 500] (cmns-moon.think)  OATMEALCAKES(M)                 USENET Cookbook    45

<space> selects, arrows move, w for keywords, s for sources, ? for help
```

4. Now you can look at the documents that WAIS found. Move the cursor to the desired document with the arrow keys or type the line number followed by Enter.
5. Press the spacebar to retrieve the document.
6. WAIS displays the document a page at a time. Press the spacebar to move from page to page or press **q** to stop displaying the document.
7. After displaying as many documents as you want, press **s** to prepare for another search, or **q** to exit.

Mailing yourself a copy

To e-mail yourself a copy of a document, press | (vertical bar) followed by **mail** *name@host* where *name@host* is your e-mail address and then press Enter. You only have to enter this information once — after that, WAIS remembers the command, so you need only press | and Enter.

See *The Internet For Dummies*, Chapter 21, section "WAIS and Means."

WAIS — Selecting Databases to Search

Telling WAIS which databases (also known as *document sources*) to look in while doing your search.

WAIS can search hundreds of different databases. The following steps tell you how to select a database to search:

1. Run WAIS as described in the section "WAIS — Searching for Text," elsewhere in this Part.

   (You may see a list of hundreds of document sources that WAIS is prepared to search — if not, see the next section, "Database of Servers" to find out how to add sources to the list.)

2. Press down-arrow or **j** (lowercase) to move down the list. Press up-arrow or **k** (lowercase) to move up the list. To move up a page at a time, press **J** (uppercase). To move down a page at a time, press **K** (uppercase).

   When you get to the end of the list, WAIS shows you the beginning again. Likewise, when you move up to the beginning, WAIS shows you the end (it's an endless loop). You can also move right to a document source on the list by pressing / (slash) followed by the name of the document source.

3. When you see a document source that might contain the information you want, select it by pressing the spacebar or **.** (period). You can select as many document sources as you want.

4. WAIS confirms that you have selected the document source by displaying an asterisk, as in the following figure. (Pressing the spacebar for a selected source deselects it.)

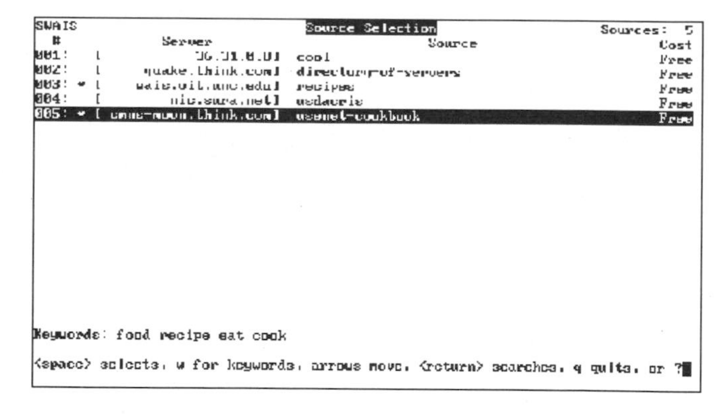

Now you are ready to tell WAIS what to search for, as described in the section "WAIS — Searching for Text in Documents," elsewhere in this Part.

Database of Servers

If you can't find any promising document sources, select the document source called *Database of Servers* and search it for more possible databases. Follow these steps:

1. Run WAIS.
2. Select the *Database of Servers* by moving the cursor to it and pressing the spacebar or **.** (period).
3. Press **w** to tell WAIS that you want to enter the text to search for.
4. Enter some words describing the kinds of topics you want.
5. Press Enter to search for document sources. WAIS gives you a chance to add more keywords — do so if you want and then press Enter to start the search.
6. WAIS finds a list of document sources. Move to an interesting one with the up- and down-arrows or type the line number followed by Enter.
7. Press the spacebar to look at the source description (the description of the document it found). If it is more than one page, press the spacebar to page through the description.

   To add the server to the list that WAIS can use, press **u**.
8. Repeat these steps for as many sources as you want.
9. Press **s** to return to the WAIS sources screen.

See The Internet For Dummies, Chapter 21, "We Have WAIS of Finding Your Information."

WINWAIS

A Microsoft Windows program that provides access to WAIS.

WINWAIS and other windowed clients require the same general steps as UNIX WAIS but are considerably easier to use. If you access the Internet via a PC running Microsoft Windows, you can install and use WINWAIS.

In WINWAIS, you perform the same sequence of steps listed above to do a search: select sources, do the search, and retrieve documents. You can optionally refine the search if you don't find just what you want.

WINWAIS — Refining the Search

Using WINWAIS's *relevance feedback.*

Relevance feedback lets you tell WAIS what kind of documents you like.

1. Perform a search as described in the other WINWAIS entries in this Part of the book.
2. Click on an appropriate document in the lower window and then drag it into the middle Similar To window, or click on Add Doc.
3. Click on Search to try the search again.

   WINWAIS looks for documents that are similar to the documents you chose.
4. To remove a document from the relevance list, click on it in the middle window and then click Delete Doc.

WINWAIS — Searching for Text

Using the WINWAIS program to search for text.

1. Run WINWAIS by double-clicking on its icon in the Windows Program Manager.
2. Follow the instructions contained in the other WINWAIS entries in this Part of this book to select document sources, enter the text you want to search for, and retrieve the documents that look interesting.
3. When you are done, choose File⇨Exit to leave WINWAIS, or press Alt+F4.

See *The Internet For Dummies*, Chapter 21, section "Windows into WAIS."

WINWAIS — Searching for Text in Documents

Telling WINWAIS what words or phrases to search for.

Note: Before you use WINWAIS to search for text within documents, be sure that you have already selected the document sources to search in.

1. In WINWAIS, return to the Sources window by clicking on the Sources button at the upper left.
2. To add new sources to the current list, double-click on them in the lower subwindow or drag them from the lower window to the upper.
3. To remove sources from the current list, double-click on them in the upper subwindow or drag them from the upper window to the lower.

   Don't forget to deselect the *Directory of Sources.*

4. Click on Done.
5. Type the search words describing the documents you want into the Tell Me About window.
6. Click on Search.

   WINWAIS retrieves matching documents, as in the following figure. The documents are scored from one star to four, with four stars being the best, depending on how well they matched.

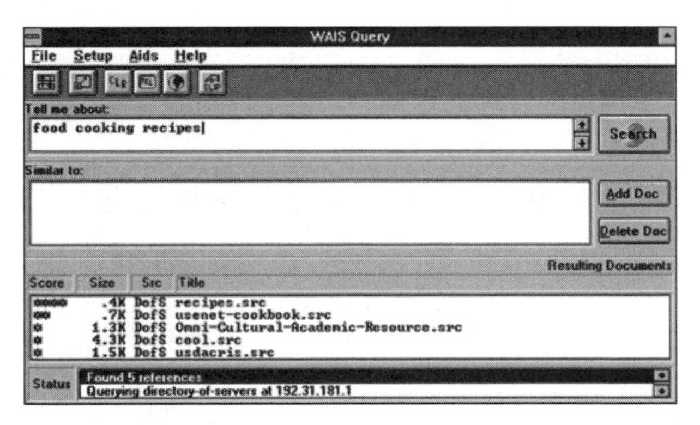

7. Double-click on a document of interest in the lower window.
8. WINWAIS displays the document, as in the following figure:

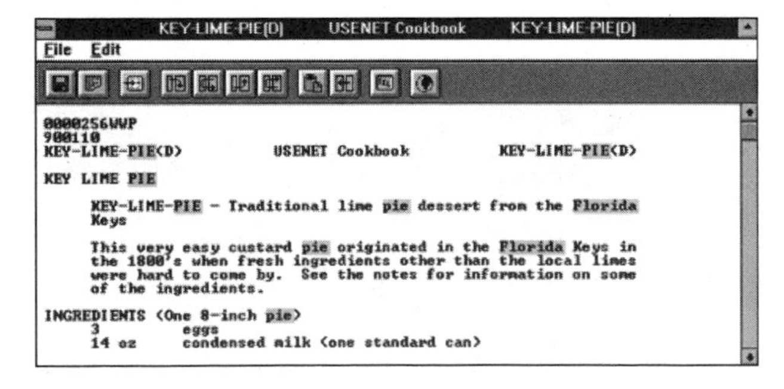

9. To save the document, click on the Save button, the one that looks like a little floppy disk. It pops up a standard filename window to let you specify the filename.
10. To print the document, click on the Print button, the one next to the Save button.
11. Close the window by double-clicking on the menu button in the upper left-hand corner of the window border.

WINWAIS — Selecting Databases to Search

Telling WINWAIS which databases (*document sources*) to look in while doing the search.

The following steps describe how to select databases for WINWAIS to search.

1. In WINWAIS, open the Sources window by clicking on the Sources button (the large button at the upper left under the File menu), as in the following figure:

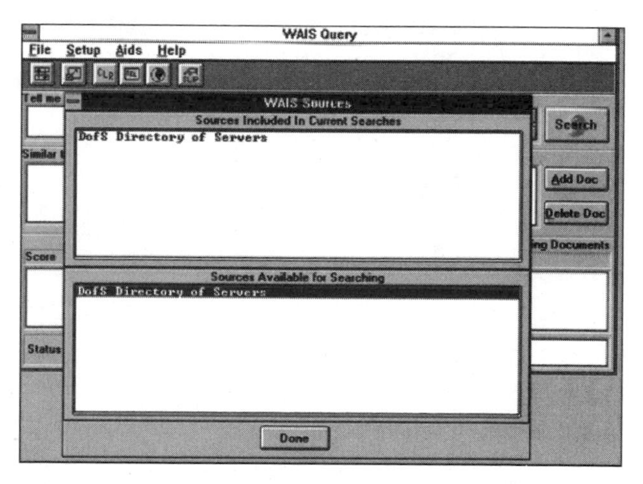

2. The upper subwindow lists sources currently in use; the lower window lists all sources available. If the *Directory of Sources* doesn't already appear in the upper window, double-click on it in the lower window to select it.
3. Click on Done to dismiss the Sources window.
4. In the upper Tell Me About window, type terms describing the kind of sources you want.

5. Click on Search to find matching sources, as in the following figure:

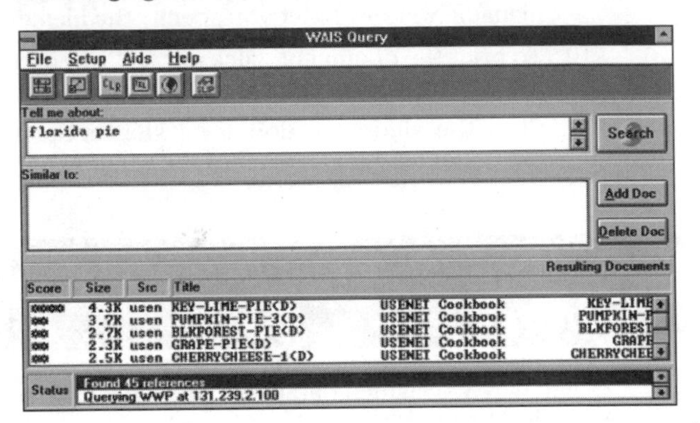

6. In the lower window, double-click on a source of interest. If the list doesn't fit in the window, use the scroll bar to scroll the list up and down.
7. WINWAIS displays information about the source, as in the following figure:

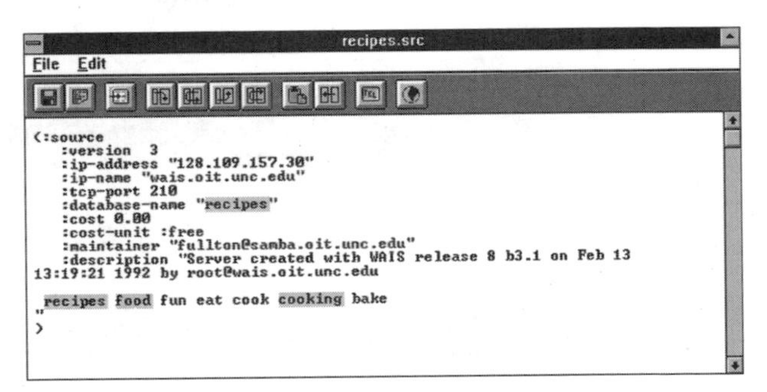

8. To add the document source to the list of known sources, click on the Save button (the little floppy disk at the top left).
9. A window pops up that lets you edit the source. Don't do any editing — click on Add and then Done to finish adding it.
10. To disregard the source, dismiss the window by double-clicking on the control menu button in the upper left-hand corner of the window border.
11. Repeat for any other document sources that look interesting.

Now you are ready to search these document sources (see the section "WINWAIS — Searching for Text in Documents," elsewhere in this Part).

World Wide Web

WWW — a *hypertext* system linking together many kinds of information all over the world.

WWW — Navigating Around

Moving through the WWW hypertext system.

WWW displays pages of information, with *links* to other pages. Here is a sample page:

```
Welcome to WWW at the University of Kansas

You are using a new WWW Product called Lynx.
For more information about obtaining
and installing Lynx please choose About Lynx
The current version of Lynx is 2.0.10. If you
are running an earlier version
PLEASE UPGRADE!

    WWW sources
For a description of WWW choose Web Overview
About the WWW Information Sharing project
WWW Information By Subject
WWW Information By Type

    Lynx sources
    University of Kansas CWIS
    History Net Archives

    Gopher sources
University of Minnesota Gopher Server (Home of
the Gopher)
All the Gopher servers in the world
```

Different systems display the links differently, by highlighting the link items or by putting a code (such as a number in brackets) after the item. In the preceding screen example, each link is displayed in boldface.

You can follow these links to see other information:

1. On a windowed, full-screen system such as Mosaic, use the mouse to click on the link.

   If the page doesn't fit on the screen, use the scroll bar to scroll up and down.

2. On a text system that highlights the links, move the cursor to the desired link with Tab and the up and down arrow keys and then press Enter.

   If the page doesn't fit on the screen, scroll up and down using the scroll bar at the side of the window.

3. On a text system that displays links as numbers in brackets, type the number followed by Enter. If the page doesn't fit on the screen, press **N** (next) or **B** (back) followed by Enter to scroll up and down.

See *The Internet For Dummies*, Chapter 22, "It's More than Super, It's Hyper: the World Wide Web."

More info

WWW can handle items other than text pages with links:

- Query items let you type in words to search for, and WWW creates a page based on the results of the search.
- File items can contain text, pictures, or sound. If your WWW program can handle the file, it displays or plays it. If not, it just tells you about it.

WWW can handle Gopher, Archie, and WAIS databases. If you have a decent WWW program such as Mosaic, you may find that it is the easiest way to access all these systems.

See *The Internet For Dummies*, Chapter 22, section "Another Way Around the Web."

WWW — Using WWW

Using the hypertext-based browsing system.

There is less WWW information available now than Gopher and WAIS information, but the information that WWW has is usefully linked together.

- If you have a local copy of Mosaic on your UNIX, Windows, or Macintosh system, it's the best way to use WWW. Run it.
- Otherwise, `telnet` to a public WWW server and log in linktoolbaras `www`.

Public WWW servers

Here is a list of servers you can use:

Server Name	Location
info.cern.ch	Switzerland
www.njit.edu	New Jersey
hnsource.cc.ukans.edu	Kansas

Each of the preceding public servers uses a different interface program, so it's worth trying each of them to see which one you like best. The information available from each of them is the same.

Appendix A

Internet Connections by Country

This Appendix contains a long list of countries and gives Internet connection information for each one. The connection information is given in code letters.

The following small table "Key to code letters" provides the key to the code letters used in the big table — the Internet "Connections by country" list which begins on the next page.

Key to code letters

Letter	Meaning
B	Full connection to BITNET network
b	Minimal connection to BITNET (five or fewer sites)
I	Connected to Internet
i	Connected to Internet, inaccessible from some networks
U	Connected to UUCP dial-up network
u	Minimal connection to UUCP (five or fewer sites)
F	Connected to FIDONET dial-up network
f	Minimal connection to FIDONET (five or fewer sites)

All the network connections listed support e-mail. Only the Internet supports other services. As you can see, many small countries in the list still have no networks at all.

Connections by country

Type of Connection	Country Code	Country
-----	AF	Afghanistan (Democratic Republic of)
-----	AL	Albania (Republic of)
-----	DZ	Algeria (People's Democratic Republic of)
-----	AS	American Samoa
-----	AD	Andorra (Principality of)
-----	AO	Angola (People's Republic of)
-----	AI	Anguilla
-I---	AQ	Antarctica
-----	AG	Antigua and Barbuda
BIUF-	AR	Argentina (Argentine Republic)
--u--	AM	Armenia
---f-	AW	Aruba
-IUFo	AU	Australia
BIUFO	AT	Austria (Republic of)
--U--	AZ	Azerbaijan
-----	BS	Bahamas (Commonwealth of the)
b----	BH	Bahrain (State of)
-----	BD	Bangladesh (People's Republic of)
--u--	BB	Barbados
--UF-	BY	Belarus
BIUFO	BE	Belgium (Kingdom of)
----	BZ	Belize
-----	BJ	Benin (People's Republic of)
--uf-	BM	Bermuda
-----	BT	Bhutan (Kingdom of)
--U--	BO	Bolivia (Republic of)
-----	BA	Bosnia-Hercegovina
--uf-	BW	Botswana (Republic of)
-----	BV	Bouvet Island
BIUFO	BR	Brazil (Federative Republic of)
-----	IO	British Indian Ocean Territory
-----	BN	Brunei Darussalam
bIUF-	BG	Bulgaria (Republic of)
--u--	BF	Burkina Faso (formerly Upper Volta)
-----	BI	Burundi (Republic of)

-----	KH	Cambodia
--u--	CM	Cameroon (Republic of)
BIUFO	CA	Canada
-----	CV	Cape Verde (Republic of)
-----	KY	Cayman Islands
-----	CF	Central African Republic
-----	TD	Chad (Republic of)
BIUF-	CL	Chile (Republic of)
--u-O	CN	China (People's Republic of)
-----	CX	Christmas Island (Indian Ocean)
-----	CC	Cocos (Keeling) Islands
B-u--	CO	Colombia (Republic of)
-----	KM	Comoros (Islamic Federal Republic of the)
--u--	CG	Congo (Republic of the)
-----	CK	Cook Islands
bIuf-	CR	Costa Rica (Republic of)
--uf-	CI	Cote d'Ivoire (Republic of)
-IuFo	HR	Croatia
--U--	CU	Cuba (Republic of)
bI--	CY	Cyprus (Republic of)
BIUF-	CZ	Czech Republic
bIUFO	DK	Denmark (Kingdom of)
-----	DJ	Djibouti (Republic of)
-----	DM	Dominica (Commonwealth of)
--Uf-	DO	Dominican Republic
-----	TP	East Timor
bIu--	EC	Ecuador (Republic of)
b-U--	EG	Egypt (Arab Republic of)
-----	SV	El Salvador (Republic of)
-----	GQ	Equatorial Guinea (Republic of)
-IUF-	EE	Estonia (Republic of)
--f-	ET	Ethiopia (People's Democratic Republic of)
-----	FK	Falkland Islands (Malvinas)
-----	FO	Faroe Islands
-Iu--	FJ	Fiji (Republic of)
BIUFO	FI	Finland (Republic of)
BIUFO	FR	France (French Republic)
--u--	GF	French Guiana
--u -	PF	French Polynesia

Type of Connection	Country Code	Country
- - - - -	TF	French Southern Territories
- - - - -	GA	Gabon (Gabonese Republic)
- - - - -	GM	Gambia (Republic of the)
- - UF -	GE	Georgia (Republic of)
BIUFO	DE	Germany (Federal Republic of)
- - F -	GH	Ghana (Republic of)
- - - - -	GI	Gibraltar
BIUFO	GR	Greece (Hellenic Republic)
-I-f-	GL	Greenland
- - u - -	GD	Grenada
b - uf -	GP	Guadeloupe (French Department of)
- - F -	GU	Guam
- - u - -	GT	Guatemala (Republic of)
- - - - -	GN	Guinea (Republic of)
- - - - -	GW	Guinea-Bissau (Republic of)
- - - - -	GY	Guyana (Republic of)
- - - - -	HT	Haiti (Republic of)
- - - - -	HM	Heard and McDonald Islands
- - - - -	HN	Honduras (Republic of)
BI - F -	HK	Hong Kong
BIUFo	HU	Hungary (Republic of)
- IUFo	IS	Iceland (Republic of)
bIUfO	IN	India (Republic of)
- - u - -	ID	Indonesia (Republic of)
b - - - -	IR	Iran (Islamic Republic of)
- - - - -	IQ	Iraq (Republic of)
BIUFO	IE	Ireland
BIUF -	IL	Israel (State of)
BIUFO	IT	Italy (Italian Republic)
- - u - -	JM	Jamaica
BIUF -	JP	Japan
- - - - -	JO	Jordan (Hashemite Kingdom of)
- - Uf -	KZ	Kazakhstan
- - f -	KE	Kenya (Republic of)
- - u - -	KI	Kiribati (Republic of)
- - - - -	KP	Korea (Democratic People's Republic of)
BIUFO	KR	Korea (Republic of)

-I--	KW	Kuwait (State of)
--U--	KG	Kyrgyzstan
-----	LA	Lao People's Democratic Republic
-IUF-	LV	Latvia (Republic of)
-----	LB	Lebanon (Lebanese Republic)
--u--	LS	Lesotho (Kingdom of)
-----	LR	Liberia (Republic of)
-----	LY	Libyan Arab Jamahiriya
--f-	LI	Liechtenstein (Principality of)
--UFo	LT	Lithuania
bIUFo	LU	Luxembourg (Grand Duchy of)
--F-	MO	Macau (Ao-me'n)
-----	??	Macedonia (Former Yugoslav Republic of)
-----	MG	Madagascar (Democratic Republic of)
--u--	MW	Malawi (Republic of)
bIUF-	MY	Malaysia
-----	MV	Maldives (Republic of)
--u--	ML	Mali (Republic of)
--u--	MT	Malta (Republic of)
-----	MH	Marshall Islands (Republic of the)
-----	MQ	Martinique (French Department of)
-----	MR	Mauritania (Islamic Republic of)
--uf-	MU	Mauritius
BIuF-	MX	Mexico (United Mexican States)
-----	FM	Micronesia (Federated States of)
--UF-	MD	Moldova (Republic of)
-----	MC	Monaco (Principality of)
-----	MN	Mongolia (Mongolian People's Republic)
-----	MS	Montserrat
-----	MA	Morocco (Kingdom of)
--u--	MZ	Mozambique (People's Republic of)
-----	MM	Myanmar (Union of)
--u--	NA	Namibia (Republic of)
-----	NR	Nauru (Republic of)
-----	NP	Nepal (Kingdom of)
BIUFO	NL	Netherlands (Kingdom of the)
-----	AN	Netherlands Antilles
-----	NT	Neutral Zone (between Saudi Arabia and Iraq)

Type of Connection	Country Code	Country
- - U - -	NC	New Caledonia
- IUF -	NZ	New Zealand
- - u - -	NI	Nicaragua (Republic of)
- - u - -	NE	Niger (Republic of the)
- - - - -	NG	Nigeria (Federal Republic of)
- - - - -	NU	Niue
- - - - -	NF	Norfolk Island
- - - - -	MP	Northern Mariana Islands (Common wealth of the)
BIUFO	NO	Norway (Kingdom of)
- - - - -	OM	Oman (Sultanate of)
- - U - -	PK	Pakistan (Islamic Republic of)
- - - - -	PW	Palau (Republic of)
b - uF -	PA	Panama (Republic of)
- - u - -	PG	Papua New Guinea
- - u - -	PY	Paraguay (Republic of)
- - Uf -	PE	Peru (Republic of)
- - uF -	PH	Philippines (Republic of the)
- - - - -	PN	Pitcairn
BIUF -	PL	Poland (Republic of)
bIUFO	PT	Portugal (Portuguese Republic)
bIUF -	PR	Puerto Rico
- - - - -	QA	Qatar (State of)
- - u - -	RE	Re'union (French Department of)
BI - f -	RO	Romania
BiUF -	RU	Russian Federation
- - - - -	RW	Rwanda (Rwandese Republic)
- - - - -	SH	Saint Helena
- - - - -	KN	Saint Kitts and Nevis
- - u - -	LC	Saint Lucia
- - - - -	PM	Saint Pierre and Miquelon (French Department of)
- - - - -	VC	Saint Vincent and the Grenadines
- - u - -	WS	Samoa (Independent State of)
- - - - -	SM	San Marino (Republic of)
- - - - -	ST	Sao Tome and Principe (Democratic Republic of)

B- - - -	SA	Saudi Arabia (Kingdom of)
- -Uf-	SN	Senegal (Republic of)
- -u- -	SC	Seychelles (Republic of)
- - - - -	SL	Sierra Leone (Republic of)
bIuF-	SG	Singapore (Republic of)
bIUF-	SK	Slovakia
-IUFO	SI	Slovenia
- -u- -	SB	Solomon Islands
- - - - -	SO	Somalia (Somali Democratic Republic)
-IUFO	ZA	South Africa (Republic of)
BIUFO	ES	Spain (Kingdom of)
- -U- -	LK	Sri Lanka (Democratic Socialist Republic of)
- - - - -	SD	Sudan (Democratic Republic of the)
- -u- -	SR	Suriname (Republic of)
- - - - -	SJ	Svalbard and Jan Mayen Islands
- -u- -	SZ	Swaziland (Kingdom of)
BIUFo	SE	Sweden (Kingdom of)
BIUFO	CH	Switzerland (Swiss Confederation)
- - - - -	SY	Syria (Syrian Arab Republic)
BIuF-	TW	Taiwan, Province of China
- -uf-	TJ	Tajikistan
- -f-	TZ	Tanzania (United Republic of)
-IUF-	TH	Thailand (Kingdom of)
- -u- -	TG	Togo (Togolese Republic)
- - - - -	TK	Tokelau
- -u- -	TO	Tonga (Kingdom of)
- -u- -	TT	Trinidad and Tobago (Republic of)
bIUfo	TN	Tunisia
BI-F-	TR	Turkey (Republic of)
- -U- -	TM	Turkmenistan
- - - - -	TC	Turks and Caicos Islands
- -u- -	TV	Tuvalu
- -f-	UG	Uganda (Republic of)
-iUF-	UA	Ukraine
- - - - -	AE	United Arab Emirates
bIUFO	GB	United Kingdom (United Kingdom of Great Britain and Northern Ireland)

Type of Connection	Country Code	Country
BIUFO	US	United States (United States of America)
- - - - -	UM	United States Minor Outlying Islands
- - UF -	UY	Uruguay (Eastern Republic of)
- - UF -	UZ	Uzbekistan
- - u - -	VU	Vanuatu (Republic of, formerly New Hebrides)
- - - - -	VA	Vatican City State (Holy See)
- IU - -	VE	Venezuela (Republic of)
- - - - -	VN	Vietnam (Socialist Republic of)
- - - - -	VG	Virgin Islands (British)
- - f -	VI	Virgin Islands (U.S.)
- - - - -	WF	Wallis and Futuna Islands
- - - - -	EH	Western Sahara
- - - - -	YE	Yemen (Republic of)
- - f -	YU	Yugoslavia (Socialist Federal Republic of)
- - - - -	ZR	Zaire (Republic of)
- - uf -	ZM	Zambia (Republic of)
- - uf -	ZW	Zimbabwe (Republic of)

Appendix B

Usenet Newsgroups by Hierarchy

See Part 3 of this book for information on subscribing and unsubscribing to Usenet newsgroups.

The following list of net news categories contains the top-level names of the "official" Usenet *hierarchies* distributed to nearly every news site:

Hierarchy	*What It Deals With*
`comp`	Topics regarding computers. Lots of fairly meaty discussions.
`misc`	Miscellaneous topics. (The ultimate miscellaneous group is `misc.misc`.)
`news`	Topics regarding net news. Although everyone should check out the few groups that include introductory material and the occasional important announcement, by and large these groups are not very interesting — unless you're a news weenie.
`rec`	Topics regarding recreation (including sports, hobbies, the arts, and other fun endeavors).
`sci`	Topics regarding the sciences — also fairly meaty.
`soc`	Social groups — both social interests and plain socializing.
`talk`	Long arguments, frequently regarding politics. Widely considered to be very boring, except by the participants.

Many more kinds of groups are less widely distributed; We list some later in this appendix.

Comp Groups

Name	Description
comp.admin.policy	Discussion of site administration policies.
comp.ai	Artificial intelligence.
comp.ai.fuzzy	Fuzzy set theory (fuzzy logic).
comp.ai.genetic	Genetic algorithms in computing.
comp.ai.jair.announce	Announcements and abstracts of the *Journal of AI Research*. (Moderated)
comp.ai.jair.papers	Papers published by the *Journal of AI Research*. (Moderated)
comp.ai.nat-lang	Natural language processing.
comp.ai.neural-nets	Neural networks.
comp.ai.nlang-know-rep	Natural Language, Knowledge Representation. (Moderated)
comp.ai.philosophy	Philosophical aspects of artificial intelligence.
comp.ai.shells	AI applied to shells.
comp.answers	Repository for Usenet articles. (Moderated)
comp.apps.spreadsheets	Spreadsheets on various platforms.
comp.arch	Computer architecture.
comp.arch.bus.vmebus	VMEbus systems (hardware and software).
comp.arch.storage	Storage system issues (hardware and software).
comp.archives	Descriptions of public access archives. (Moderated)
comp.archives.admin	Issues related to computer archive administration.
comp.archives.msdos.announce	Announcements about MS-DOS archives. (Moderated)
comp.archives.msdos.d	Materials in MS-DOS archives.
comp.bbs.misc	Bulletin board systems.
comp.bbs.waffle	The Waffle BBS and USENET system, on all platforms.
comp.benchmarks	Benchmarking techniques and results.

comp.binaries.acorn	Binary-only postings for Acorn machines. (Moderated)
comp.binaries.amiga	Encoded public domain programs in binary. (Moderated)
comp.binaries.apple2	Binary-only postings for Apple II.
comp.binaries.atari.st	Binary-only postings for the Atari ST. (Moderated)
comp.binaries.cbm	For the transfer of 8bit Commodore binaries. (Moderated)
comp.binaries.ibm.pc	Binary-only postings for IBM PC/MS-DOS. (Moderated)
comp.binaries.ibm.pc.d	Discussion of IBM PC binary postings.
comp.binaries.ibm.pc.wanted	Requests for IBM PC and compatible programs.
comp.binaries.mac	Encoded Macintosh programs in binary. (Moderated)
comp.binaries.ms-windows	Binary programs for Microsoft Windows. (Moderated)
comp.binaries.os2	Binaries for use under the OS/2 ABI. (Moderated)
comp.bugs.2bsd	Reports of UNIX version 2BSD-related bugs.
comp.bugs.4bsd	Reports of UNIX version 4BSD-related bugs.
comp.bugs.4bsd.ucb-fixes	Bug reports/fixes for BSD UNIX. (Moderated)
comp.bugs.misc	General UNIX bug reports and fixes (including V7, UUCP).
comp.bugs.sys5	Bug reports for USG (System III, V, and so on).
comp.cad.cadence	Users of Cadence Design Systems products.
comp.cad.compass	Compass Design Automation EDA tools.
comp.cad.pro-engineer	Parametric Technology's Pro/Engineer design package.
comp.cad.synthesis	Research and production in logic synthesis.
comp.client-server	Topics, client/server technology.
comp.cog-eng	Cognitive engineering.
comp.compilers	Compiler construction, theory, and so on. (Moderated)

Name	Description
comp.compression	Data compression algorithms and theory.
comp.compression.research	Data compression research. (Moderated)
comp.databases	Database and data management — issues and theory.
comp.databases.informix	Informix database management software.
comp.databases.ingres	Issues related to INGRES products.
comp.databases.ms-access	Issues related to Microsoft Access, the relational database system for Microsoft Windows.
comp.databases.object	Object-oriented paradigms in database systems.
comp.databases.oracle	The SQL database products of Oracle Corp.
comp.databases.paradox	Issues related to Paradox, Borland's database for DOS and Microsoft Windows.
comp.databases.pick	Pick-like, post-relational database systems.
comp.databases.rdb	Relational database engine Rdb from DEC.
comp.databases.sybase	Implementations, SQL Server.
comp.databases.theory	Discussion of advances in database technology.
comp.databases.xbase.fox	Fox Software's Xbase (dBASE-like) and compatibles.
comp.databases.xbase.misc	xBase products.
comp.dcom.cell-relay	Cell Relay-based products.
comp.dcom.fax	Fax hardware, software, protocols.
comp.dcom.isdn	Integrated Services Digital Network (ISDN).
comp.dcom.lans.ethernet	Discussion of Ethernet/IEEE 802.3 protocols.
comp.dcom.lans.fddi	Discussion of FDDI protocol suite.
comp.dcom.lans.misc	Local area network (hardware and software).

comp.dcom.lans.token-ring	Token ring networks.
comp.dcom.modems	Data communications (hardware and software).
comp.dcom.servers	Selecting and operating data communications servers.
comp.dcom.sys.cisco	Cisco routers and bridges.
comp.dcom.sys.wellfleet	Wellfleet bridge & router systems (hardware & software).
comp.dcom.telecom	Telecommunications digest. (Moderated)
comp.dcom.telecom.tech	Technical aspects of telephony.
comp.doc	Archived public-domain documentation. (Moderated)
comp.doc.techreports	Lists of technical reports. (Moderated)
comp.dsp	Digital Signal Processing using computers.
comp.edu	Computer science education.
comp.emacs	EMACS editors..
comp.fonts	Type fonts — design, conversion, use, and so on.
comp.graphics	Computer graphics, art, animation, image processing.
comp.graphics.algorithms	Algorithms used to produce computer graphics.
comp.graphics.animation	Technical aspects of computer animation.
comp.graphics.avs	Application Visualization System.
comp.graphics.data-explorer	IBM's Visualization Data Explorer, a.k.a. DX.
comp.graphics.explorer	Explorer Modular Visualization Environment (MVE).
comp.graphics.gnuplot	GNUPLOT interactive function plotter.
comp.graphics.opengl	OpenGL 3-D application programming interface.
comp.graphics.research	Highly technical computer graphics discussion. (Moderated)
comp.groupware	Shared interactive environments (hardware and software).
comp.human-factors	Issues related to human-computer interaction (HCI).

Name	Description
comp.infosystems	Information systems.
comp.infosystems.announce	Announcements of Internet information services. (Moderated)
comp.infosystems.gis	Geographic Information Systems.
comp.infosystems.gopher	Gopher information service.
comp.infosystems.wais	Z39.50-based WAIS full-text search system.
comp.infosystems.www	World Wide Web.
comp.internet.library	Electronic libraries. (Moderated)
comp.ivideodisc	Interactive videodiscs.
comp.lang.ada	Ada.
comp.lang.apl	APL.
comp.lang.basic.misc	Other BASIC dialects, aspects.
comp.lang.basic.visual	Microsoft's Visual Basic and Applications Basic (Windows and DOS).
comp.lang.c	C.
comp.lang.c++	C++ (object-oriented language).
comp.lang.clos	Common Lisp Object System.
comp.lang.dylan	Dylan (language).
comp.lang.eiffel	Eiffel (object-oriented language).
comp.lang.forth	FORTH.
comp.lang.fortran	FORTRAN.
comp.lang.functional	Functional languages.
comp.lang.hermes	Hermes (language for distributed applications).
comp.lang.idl-pvwave	IDL and PV-Wave language.
comp.lang.lisp	LISP.
comp.lang.lisp.mcl	Apple's Macintosh Common Lisp.
comp.lang.logo	LOGO (teaching and learning language).
comp.lang.misc	Other computer languages.
comp.lang.ml	ML languages, including Standard ML, CAML, Lazy ML, and so on. (Moderated)
comp.lang.modula2	Modula-2.
comp.lang.modula3	Modula-3.
comp.lang.oberon	Oberon language and system.
comp.lang.objective-c	Objective-C language and environment.

comp.lang.pascal	Pascal.
comp.lang.perl	Larry Wall's Perl system.
comp.lang.pop	Pop11 and the Plug user group.
comp.lang.postscript	PostScript (page description language).
comp.lang.prolog	Prolog.
comp.lang.sather	Sather (object-oriented language).
comp.lang.scheme	Scheme (programming language).
comp.lang.sigplan	Information and announcements from ACM SIGPLAN. (Moderated)
comp.lang.smalltalk	Smalltalk 80.
comp.lang.tcl	Tcl (programming language and related tools).
comp.lang.verilog	Verilog and PLI.
comp.lang.vhdl	VHSIC Hardware Description Language, IEEE 1076/87.
comp.laser-printers	Laser printers (hardware and software). (Moderated)
comp.lsi	Large-scale integrated circuits.
comp.lsi.testing	Testing of electronic circuits.
comp.mail.elm	Discussion, fixes for elm mail system.
comp.mail.headers	Gatewayed from the Internet header-people list.
comp.mail.maps	Various maps, including UUCP maps. (Moderated)
comp.mail.mh	UCI version of the Rand Message Handling system.
comp.mail.mime	Multipurpose Internet mail extensions of RFC 1341.
comp.mail.misc	Discussion of computer mail.
comp.mail.mush	The Mail User's Shell (MUSH).
comp.mail.sendmail	The BSD sendmail agent.
comp.mail.uucp	Mail in the UUCP environment.
comp.misc	General topics regarding computers.
comp.multimedia	Interactive multimedia technologies.
comp.newprod	Announcements of new products. (Moderated)
comp.object	Object-oriented programming.
comp.object.logic	Integrating object-oriented and logic programming.

Name	Description
comp.org.acm	Topics regarding the Association for Computing Machinery.
comp.org.decus	Digital Equipment Computer Users' Society newsgroup.
comp.org.eff.news	News from the Electronic Frontier Foundation. (Moderated)
comp.org.eff.talk	EFF goals, strategies, and so on.
comp.org.fidonet	FidoNews digest, official news of FIDONET Assoc. (Moderated)
comp.org.ieee	Issues and announcements about IEEE and its members.
comp.org.issnnet	International Student Society for Neural Networks.
comp.org.lisp-users	Association of LISP Users.
comp.org.sug	Sun User's Group.
comp.org.usenix	USENIX Association events and announcements.
comp.org.usenix.roomshare	Lodging during USENIX conferences.
comp.os.386bsd.announce	Announcements regarding 386bsd operating system. (Moderated)
comp.os.386bsd.apps	Applications that run under 386bsd.
comp.os.386bsd.bugs	Bugs, fixes for 386bsd OS and clients.
comp.os.386bsd.development	Working on 386bsd internals.
comp.os.386bsd.misc	Aspects of 386bsd not covered by other groups.
comp.os.386bsd.questions	Questions about 386bsd.
comp.os.coherent	Coherent (operating system).
comp.os.cpm	CP/M (operating system).
comp.os.geos	GEOS (OS by GeoWorks for PCs).
comp.os.linux.admin	Installing and administering Linux systems.
comp.os.linux.announce	Announcements important to the Linux community. (Moderated)
comp.os.linux.development	Ongoing Linux development.
comp.os.linux.help	Questions and advice regarding Linux.

comp.os.linux.misc	Other Linux-specific topics.
comp.os.lynx	LynxOS and Lynx Real-Time systems.
comp.os.mach	MACH OS from CMU and other places.
comp.os.minix	Andrew Tannenbaum's MINIX system.
comp.os.misc	General OS-oriented discussion.
comp.os.ms-windows.advocacy	Speculation and debate about Microsoft Windows.
comp.os.ms-windows.announce	Announcements related to Microsoft Windows. (Moderated)
comp.os.ms-windows.apps	Applications in MS-Windows.
comp.os.ms-windows.misc	General discussion of Microsoft Windows.
comp.os.ms-windows.nt.misc	General discussion of Microsoft Windows NT.
comp.os.ms-windows.nt.setup	Configuring Microsoft Windows NT systems.
comp.os.ms-windows.programmer.misc	Programming Microsoft Windows.
comp.os.ms-windows.programmer.tools	Microsoft Windows develop ment tools.
comp.os.ms-windows.programmer.win32	32-bit Microsoft Windows programming interfaces.
comp.os.ms-windows.setup	Installing and configuring Microsoft Windows.
comp.os.msdos.apps	Applications under MS-DOS.
comp.os.msdos.desqview	QuarterDeck's DESQview and related products.
comp.os.msdos.mail-news	Administering mail and network news systems under MS-DOS.
comp.os.msdos.misc	Miscellaneous topics regarding MS-DOS machines.
comp.os.msdos.pcgeos	GeoWorks PC/GEOS and PC/GEOS-based packages.
comp.os.msdos.programmer	Programming MS-DOS machines.
comp.os.msdos.programmer.turbovision	Borland's text application libraries.
comp.os.os2.advocacy	Supporting and flaming OS/2.
comp.os.os2.announce	News and announcements related to OS/2. (Moderated)

Name	Description
comp.os.os2.apps	Applications under OS/2.
comp.os.os2.beta	Beta releases of OS/2 .
comp.os.os2.bugs	Bug reports, fixes, and workarounds for OS/2 systems.
comp.os.os2.misc	Miscellaneous OS/2 topics.
comp.os.os2.multimedia	Multimedia on OS/2 systems.
comp.os.os2.networking	Networking in OS/2 environments.
comp.os.os2.programmer.misc	Programming OS/2 machines.
comp.os.os2.programmer.porting	Porting software to OS/2.
comp.os.os2.setup	Installing and configuring OS/2.
comp.os.os2.ver1x	OS/2 (Versions 1.0 through 1.3).
comp.os.os9	OS/9 (UNIX-like realtime operating system).
comp.os.qnx	Using and developing under the QNX operating system.
comp.os.research	Operating systems and related areas. (Moderated)
comp.os.vms	DEC's VAX computer family and VMS.
comp.os.vxworks	VxWorks (realtime OS).
comp.os.xinu	XINU (operating system from Purdue Univ., D. Comer).
comp.parallel	Massively parallel hardware/ software. (Moderated)
comp.parallel.pvm	PVM system of multicomputer parallelization.
comp.patents	Patents of computer technology. (Moderated)
comp.periphs	Peripheral devices.
comp.periphs.scsi	SCSI-based peripheral devices.
comp.programming	Programming issues transcending languages and OS.
comp.programming.literate	Literate programs and programming tools.
comp.protocols.appletalk	Applebus hardware, software.
comp.protocols.dicom	Digital Imaging and Communications in Medicine.
comp.protocols.ibm	Networking, IBM mainframes.
comp.protocols.iso	ISO protocol stack.
comp.protocols.kerberos	Kerberos (authentication server).

comp.protocols.kermit	Kermit. (Moderated)
comp.protocols.misc	Various types of protocols.
comp.protocols.nfs	Network File System protocol.
comp.protocols.ppp	Internet's Point to Point Protocol.
comp.protocols.tcp-ip	TCP and IP network protocols.
comp.protocols.tcp-ip.ibmpc	TCP/IP for PCs, and compatibles.
comp.publish.cdrom.hardware	Hardware for publishing with CD-ROM.
comp.publish.cdrom.multimedia	Software for multimedia authoring and publishing.
comp.publish.cdrom.software	Software for publishing with CD-ROM.
comp.realtime	Issues of realtime computing.
comp.research.japan	Research in Japan. (Moderated)
comp.risks	Risks to the public from computers and users. (Moderated)
comp.robotics	Robots and their applications.
comp.security.misc	Security issues related to computers and networks.
comp.security.unix	UNIX security.
comp.simulation	Simulation methods, problems, uses. (Moderated)
comp.society	Impact of technology on society. (Moderated)
comp.society.cu-digest	Computer Underground Digest. (Moderated)
comp.society.development	Computer technology in developing countries.
comp.society.folklore	Computer folklore and culture, past and present. (Moderated)
comp.society.futures	Events in technology affecting future computing.
comp.society.privacy	Effects of technology on privacy. (Moderated)
comp.soft-sys.khoros	Khoros X11 (visualization system).
comp.soft-sys.matlab	MathWorks (calculation and visualization package).
comp.soft-sys.sas	SAS (statistics package).
comp.soft-sys.shazam	SHAZAM (econometrics computer program).
comp.soft-sys.spss	SPSS (statistics package).

Name	Description
comp.soft-sys.wavefront	Wavefront software products, problems, and so on.
comp.software-eng	Software engineering and related topics.
comp.software.licensing	Software licensing technology.
comp.software.testing	Testing computer systems.
comp.sources.3b1	Source code-only postings for the AT&T 3b1. (Moderated)
comp.sources.acorn	Source code-only postings for the Acorn. (Moderated)
comp.sources.amiga	Source code-only postings for the Amiga. (Moderated)
comp.sources.apple2	Source code and discussion for the Apple II. (Moderated)
comp.sources.atari.st	Source code-only postings for the Atari ST. (Moderated)
comp.sources.bugs	Bug reports, fixes, and discussion for posted sources.
comp.sources.d	Discussion of source postings.
comp.sources.games	Postings of recreational software. (Moderated)
comp.sources.games.bugs	Bug reports and fixes for posted game software.
comp.sources.hp48	Programs for the HP48 and HP28 calculators. (Moderated)
comp.sources.mac	Software for the Macintosh. (Moderated)
comp.sources.misc	Postings of software. (Moderated)
comp.sources.postscript	Source code for programs written in PostScript. (Moderated)
comp.sources.reviewed	Source code evaluated by peer review. (Moderated)
comp.sources.sun	Software for Sun workstations. (Moderated)
comp.sources.testers	Finding people to test software.
comp.sources.unix	Postings of complete UNIX-oriented sources. (Moderated)
comp.sources.wanted	Requests for software and fixes.
comp.sources.x	Software for the X Window system. (Moderated)

comp.specification	Languages and methodologies for formal specification.
comp.specification.z	Z (formal specification notation).
comp.speech	Research and applications in speech science and technology.
comp.std.c	C language standards.
comp.std.c++	C++ language, library, standards.
comp.std.internat	International standards.
comp.std.lisp	User group (ALU) supported standards. (Moderated)
comp.std.misc	Discussion about various standards.
comp.std.mumps	X11.1 committee on MUMPS. (Moderated)
comp.std.unix	P1003 committee on UNIX. (Moderated)
comp.std.wireless	Examining standards for wireless network technology. (Moderated)
comp.sw.components	Software components and related technology.
comp.sys.3b1	AT&T 7300/3B1/UnixPC.
comp.sys.acorn	Acorn and ARM-based computers.
comp.sys.acorn.advocacy	Why Acorn computers and programs are better.
comp.sys.acorn.announce	Announcements for Acorn and ARM users. (Moderated)
comp.sys.acorn.tech	Acorn and ARM products (hardware and software).
comp.sys.alliant	Alliant computers.
comp.sys.amiga.advocacy	Why an Amiga is better than XYZ.
comp.sys.amiga.announce	Announcements about Amiga. (Moderated)
comp.sys.amiga.applications	Miscellaneous applications.
comp.sys.amiga.audio	Music, MIDI, speech synthesis, other sounds.
comp.sys.amiga.datacomm	Ways to get bytes in and out.
comp.sys.amiga.emulations	Various hardware and software emulators.
comp.sys.amiga.games	Discussion of games for Amiga.

comp.sys.amiga.graphics	Charts, graphs, pictures, and so on.
comp.sys.amiga.hardware	Amiga computer hardware, questions and answers, reviews, and so on.
comp.sys.amiga.introduction	Amiga newcomers.
comp.sys.amiga.marketplace	Where to find Amigas, prices, and so on.
comp.sys.amiga.misc	Topics not covered by other Amiga groups.
comp.sys.amiga.multimedia	Animations, video, and multimedia.
comp.sys.amiga.programmer	Developers and hobbyists discuss code.
comp.sys.amiga.reviews	Reviews of Amiga hardware and software. (Moderated)
comp.sys.apollo	Apollo computer systems.
comp.sys.apple2	Apple II micros.
comp.sys.apple2.comm	Apple II data communications.
comp.sys.apple2.gno	AppleIIgs GNO multitasking environment.
comp.sys.apple2.marketplace	Buying, selling, and trading Apple II equipment.
comp.sys.apple2.programmer	Programming on the Apple II.
comp.sys.apple2.usergroups	All about Apple II user groups.
comp.sys.atari.8bit	8-bit Atari micros.
comp.sys.atari.advocacy	Attacking and defending Atari computers.
comp.sys.atari.st	16-bit Atari micros.
comp.sys.atari.st.tech	Atari ST hardware and software.
comp.sys.att	AT&T micros.
comp.sys.cbm	Commodore micros.
comp.sys.concurrent	Concurrent/Masscomp line of computers. (Moderated)
comp.sys.convex	Convex computer systems hardware and software.
comp.sys.dec	DEC computer systems.
comp.sys.dec.micro	DEC micros (Rainbow, Professional 350/380)
comp.sys.encore	Encore's MultiMax computers.
comp.sys.harris	Harris computer systems, especially realtime systems.

comp.sys.hp	Hewlett-Packard equipment.
comp.sys.hp.apps	Software and applications on all HP platforms.
comp.sys.hp.hardware	Hewlett-Packard system hardware.
comp.sys.hp.hpux	Issues related to HP-UX and 9000 series computers.
comp.sys.hp.misc	Issues not covered by any other Hewlett-Packard group.
comp.sys.hp.mpe	Issues related to MPE and 3000 series computers.
comp.sys.hp48	HP48 and HP28 calculators.
comp.sys.ibm.pc.demos	Demonstration programs that showcase programmer skill.
comp.sys.ibm.pc.digest	The IBM PC, PC-XT, and PC-AT. (Moderated)
comp.sys.ibm.pc.games.action	Arcade-style games on PCs.
comp.sys.ibm.pc.games.adventure	Adventure (non-rpg) games on PCs.
comp.sys.ibm.pc.games.announce	Announcements for all PC gamers. (Moderated)
comp.sys.ibm.pc.games.flight-sim	Flight simulators on PCs.
comp.sys.ibm.pc.games.misc	Games not covered by other PC groups.
comp.sys.ibm.pc.games.rpg	Role-playing games on PCs.
comp.sys.ibm.pc.games.strategic	Strategy/planning games on PCs.
comp.sys.ibm.pc.hardware	XT/AT/EISA hardware, any vendor.
comp.sys.ibm.pc.hardware.cd-rom	CD-ROM drives and interfaces for the PC.
comp.sys.ibm.pc.hardware.chips	Processor, cache, memory chips, and so on.
comp.sys.ibm.pc.hardware.comm	Modems and communication cards for PCs.
comp.sys.ibm.pc.hardware.misc	Miscellaneous PC hardware topics.
comp.sys.ibm.pc.hardware. equipnetworking	Network hardware and ment for PCs.
comp.sys.ibm.pc.hardware.storage	Hard drives and other PC storage devices.

Name	Description
comp.sys.ibm.pc.hardware.system	Whole IBM PC computer and sclone systems.
comp.sys.ibm.pc.hardware.video	Video cards and monitors for PCs.
comp.sys.ibm.pc.misc	Discussion of IBM PCs.
comp.sys.ibm.pc.rt	Topics related to IBM's RT computer.
comp.sys.ibm.pc.soundcard	PC sound cards (hardware and software).
comp.sys.ibm.ps2.hardware	Microchannel hardware, any vendor.
comp.sys.intel	Intel systems and parts.
comp.sys.isis	ISIS distributed system (from Cornell Univ.).
comp.sys.laptops	Laptop (portable) computers.
comp.sys.m6809	6809.
comp.sys.m68k	68K.
comp.sys.m68k.pc	68K-based PCs. (Moderated)
comp.sys.m88k	88K-based computers.
comp.sys.mac.advocacy	Comparing Macintoshes to other computers.
comp.sys.mac.announce	Notices for Macintosh users. (Moderated)
comp.sys.mac.apps	Macintosh applications.
comp.sys.mac.comm	Macintosh communications.
comp.sys.mac.databases	Database systems for Macintosh.
comp.sys.mac.digest	Macintosh information and uses (but no programs). (Moderated)
comp.sys.mac.games	Macintosh games.
comp.sys.mac.graphics	Macintosh graphics: paint, draw, 3-D, CAD, animation.
comp.sys.mac.hardware	Issues related to Macintosh hardware.
comp.sys.mac.hypercard	Macintosh Hypercard information and uses.
comp.sys.mac.misc	General discussion of Macintosh.
comp.sys.mac.oop.macapp3	MacApp, Version 3 (object-oriented system).

comp.sys.mac.oop.misc	Object-oriented programming on the Macintosh.
comp.sys.mac.oop.tcl	Symantec's THINK Class Library for object programming.
comp.sys.mac.portables	Laptop Macintoshes.
comp.sys.mac.programmer	Programming Macintoshes.
comp.sys.mac.scitech	Using the Macintosh in scientific and technological work.
comp.sys.mac.system	Macintosh system software.
comp.sys.mac.wanted	Postings of "I want XYZ for my Mac."
comp.sys.mentor	Mentor Graphics products and the Silicon Compiler System.
comp.sys.mips	Systems based on MIPS chips.
comp.sys.misc	Discussion of all kinds of computers.
comp.sys.ncr	NCR computers.
comp.sys.newton.announce	Newton information postings. (Moderated)
comp.sys.newton.misc	Discussion of Newton systems.
comp.sys.newton.programmer	Newton software development.
comp.sys.next.advocacy	The NeXT religion.
comp.sys.next.announce	Announcements related to NeXT. (Moderated)
comp.sys.next.bugs	Discussion of and solutions for known NeXT bugs.
comp.sys.next.hardware	Physical aspects of NeXT computers.
comp.sys.next.marketplace	NeXT hardware, software, and jobs.
comp.sys.next.misc	General discussion of NeXT.
comp.sys.next.programmer	NeXT-related programming issues.
comp.sys.next.software	Function, use, and availability of NeXT programs.
comp.sys.next.sysadmin	NeXT system administration.
comp.sys.novell	Novell NetWare products.
comp.sys.nsc.32k	National Semiconductor 32000 series chips.
comp.sys.palmtops	Superpowered calculators that sit in your palm.

Name	Description
comp.sys.pen	Interacting with computers through pen gestures.
comp.sys.powerpc	PowerPCs.
comp.sys.prime	Prime Computer products.
comp.sys.proteon	Proteon gateway products.
comp.sys.psion	PSION Personal Computers and Organizers.
comp.sys.pyramid	Pyramid 90x computers.
comp.sys.ridge	Ridge 32 computers and ROS.
comp.sys.sequent	Sequent systems (Balance and Symmetry).
comp.sys.sgi.admin	SGI system administration.
comp.sys.sgi.announce	Announcements for the SGI community. (Moderated)
comp.sys.sgi.apps	Applications that run on the Iris.
comp.sys.sgi.bugs	Bugs found in the IRIX operating system.
comp.sys.sgi.graphics	Graphics packages and issues on SGI machines.
comp.sys.sgi.hardware	Base systems and peripherals for Iris computers.
comp.sys.sgi.misc	General discussion about Silicon Graphics' machines.
comp.sys.sinclair	Sinclair computers — for example, the ZX81, Spectrum, and QL.
comp.sys.stratus	Stratus products, including System/88, CPS-32, VOS, and FTX.
comp.sys.sun.admin	Sun system administration.
comp.sys.sun.announce	Sun announcements and Sunergy mailings. (Moderated)
comp.sys.sun.apps	Software applications for Sun computer systems.
comp.sys.sun.hardware	Sun Microsystems hardware.
comp.sys.sun.misc	Discussion about Sun products.
comp.sys.sun.wanted	People looking for Sun products and support.
comp.sys.tahoe	CCI 6/32, Harris HCX/7, and Sperry 7000 computers.

comp.sys.tandy	Tandy computers, new and old.
comp.sys.ti	Texas Instruments.
comp.sys.transputer	Transputer computer and occam language.
comp.sys.unisys	Sperry, Burroughs, Convergent, and Unisys* systems.
comp.sys.xerox	Xerox 1100 workstations and protocols.
comp.sys.zenith.z100	Zenith Z-100 (Heath H-100) computer family.
comp.terminals	Terminals.
comp.text	Text processing issues and methods.
comp.text.desktop	Technology and techniques of desktop publishing.
comp.text.frame	FrameMaker (desktop publishing).
comp.text.interleaf	Interleaf software, applications and use.
comp.text.sgml	ISO 8879 SGML, structured documents, markup languages.
comp.text.tex	TeX and LaTeX systems and macros.
comp.theory.info-retrieval	Information retrieval topics. (Moderated)
comp.unix.admin	Administering a UNIX-based system.
comp.unix.advocacy	Arguments for and against UNIX and UNIX versions.
comp.unix.aix	IBM's version of UNIX.
comp.unix.amiga	MINIX, SYSV4, and other *nix on an Amiga.
comp.unix.aux	UNIX for Macintosh II computers.
comp.unix.bsd	Berkeley Software Distribution UNIX.
comp.unix.dos-under-unix	MS-DOS running under UNIX.
comp.unix.internals	Hacking UNIX internals.
comp.unix.large	UNIX on mainframes and in large networks.
comp.unix.misc	UNIX topics not covered by other groups.
comp.unix.osf.misc	Open Software Foundation products.

Name	Description
comp.unix.osf.osf1	OSF/1.
comp.unix.pc-clone.16bit	UNIX on 286 architectures.
comp.unix.pc-clone.32bit	UNIX on 386 and 486 architectures.
comp.unix.programmer	Programming under UNIX.
comp.unix.questions	UNIX neophytes group.
comp.unix.shell	Using and programming the UNIX shell.
comp.unix.sys3	System III UNIX.
comp.unix.sys5.misc	Versions of System V that predate Release 3.
comp.unix.sys5.r3	System V Release 3.
comp.unix.sys5.r4	System V Release 4.
comp.unix.ultrix	DEC's ULTRIX.
comp.unix.unixware	Novell's UnixWare products.
comp.unix.user-friendly	Discussion of UNIX user-friendliness.
comp.unix.wizards	For UNIX wizards. (Moderated)
comp.unix.xenix.misc	Discussion of XENIX (except SCO).
comp.unix.xenix.sco	XENIX versions from the Santa Cruz Operation.
comp.virus	Computer viruses and security. (Moderated)
comp.windows.garnet	Garnet user interface development environment.
comp.windows.interviews	InterViews object-oriented window system.
comp.windows.misc	Various issues regarding window systems.
comp.windows.news	Sun Microsystems' NeWS window system.
comp.windows.open-look	Open Look GUI.
comp.windows.suit	SUIT user-interface toolkit.
comp.windows.x	X Window system.
comp.windows.x.apps	Applications for X, getting and using (but not programming).
comp.windows.x.i386unix	XFree86 window system and others.
comp.windows.x.intrinsics	X toolkit.
comp.windows.x.pex	PHIGS extension of X Window.

Misc Groups

Name	Description
misc.activism.progressive	Information for Progressive activists. (Moderated)
misc.answers	Repository for USENET articles. (Moderated)
misc.books.technical	Discussion of books about technical topics.
misc.consumers	Consumer interests, product reviews, and so on.
misc.consumers.house	Discussion about owning and maintaining a house.
misc.education	Discussion of the educational system.
misc.education.language.english	Teaching English to speakers of other languages.
misc.emerg-services	Forum for paramedics and other first responders.
misc.entrepreneurs	Discussion about operating a business.
misc.fitness	Physical fitness, exercise, bodybuilding, and so on.
misc.forsale	Items for sale.
misc.forsale.computers.d	Discussion of misc.forsale.computers.*.
misc.forsale.computers.mac	Macintosh-related computer items.
misc.forsale.computers.other	Miscellaneous computer stuff.
misc.forsale.computers.pc-clone	IBM PC-related computer items.
misc.forsale.computers.workstation	Workstation-related computer items.
misc.handicap	For/about the handicapped. (Moderated)
misc.headlines	Current interest: drug testing, terrorism, and so on.
misc.health.alternative	Alternative, complementary, and holistic health care.
misc.health.diabetes	Day-to-day diabetes management.

Name	*Description*
misc.int-property	Discussion of intellectual property rights.
misc.invest	Investments.
misc.invest.canada	Investing in Canadian financial markets.
misc.invest.funds	Bond, stock, and real estate funds.
misc.invest.real-estate	Property investments.
misc.invest.stocks	Stocks and options.
misc.invest.technical	Analyzing market trends with technical methods.
misc.jobs.contract	Discussion of contract labor.
misc.jobs.misc	Discussion of employment, workplaces, careers.
misc.jobs.offered	Positions available.
misc.jobs.offered.entry	Entry-level job listings.
misc.jobs.resumes	Resumes and "situation wanted" articles.
misc.kids	Children, behavior and activities.
misc.kids.computer	Children, using computers.
misc.kids.vacation	Discussion of family-oriented vacationing.
misc.legal	Legalities and the ethics of law.
misc.legal.computing	Legal climate of the computing world.
misc.legal.moderated	Law. (Moderated)
misc.misc	Discussions that do not fit any other group.
misc.news.east-europe.rferl	Radio Free Europe/Radio Liberty daily report. (Moderated)
misc.news.southasia	News from Bangladesh, India, Nepal, and so on. (Moderated)
misc.rural	Issues regarding rural living.
misc.taxes	Tax laws and advice.
misc.test	For testing of network software. Very boring.
misc.wanted	Requests for things wanted (*not* software).
misc.writing	Discussion of writing.

News Groups

Name	Description
news.admin.misc	Network news administration topics.
news.admin.policy	USENET policy issues.
news.admin.technical	Technical aspects of maintaining network news. (Moderated)
news.announce.conferences	Calls for papers and conference announcements. (Moderated)
news.announce.important	General announcements. (Moderated)
news.announce.newgroups	Calls for and announcements of new groups. (Moderated)
news.announce.newusers	Explanatory postings for new users. (Moderated)
news.answers	Repository for USENET articles. (Moderated)
news.config	Postings of system down times and interruptions.
news.future	Future technology of network news systems.
news.groups	Discussion and lists of newsgroups.
news.lists	News-related statistics and lists. (Moderated)
news.lists.ps-maps	Maps related to USENET traffic flows. (Moderated)
news.misc	Discussion of USENET.
news.newsites	Announcements of new sites.
news.newusers.questions	Questions and answers for new USENET users.
news.software.anu-news	VMS B-news software from Australian National Univ.
news.software.b	B-news-compatible software.
news.software.nn	“nn” news reader package.
news.software.notes	Notesfile software (Univ. of Illinois).
news.software.readers	Discussion of software used to read network news.

Rec Groups

Name	Description
rec.answers	Repository for USENET articles. (Moderated)
rec.antiques	Antiques and vintage items.
rec.aquaria	Keeping fish and aquaria.
rec.arts.animation	Animation.
rec.arts.anime	Japanese animation discussion.
rec.arts.anime.info	Announcements about Japanese animation. (Moderated)
rec.arts.anime.marketplace	Things for sale in Japanese animation world.
rec.arts.anime.stories	Japanese comic fanzines. (Moderated)
rec.arts.bodyart	Tattoos and body decoration.
rec.arts.bonsai	Dwarfish trees and shrubbery.
rec.arts.books	Books and the publishing industry.
rec.arts.books.tolkien	Works of J.R.R. Tolkien.
rec.arts.cinema	Art of cinema. (Moderated)
rec.arts.comics.info	Reviews, convention information, and other comics news. (Moderated)
rec.arts.comics.marketplace	Exchange of comics and comics-related items.
rec.arts.comics.misc	Comic books, graphic novels, sequential art.
rec.arts.comics.strips	Short-form comics.
rec.arts.comics.xbooks	Mutant Universe of Marvel Comics.
rec.arts.dance	Aspects of dance not covered by other groups.
rec.arts.disney	Disney-related subjects.
rec.arts.drwho	Dr. Who.
rec.arts.erotica	Erotic fiction and verse. (Moderated)

rec.arts.fine	Fine arts and artists.
rec.arts.int-fiction	Discussion of interactive fiction.
rec.arts.manga	Japanese storytelling.
rec.arts.marching.drumcorps	Drum and bugle corps.
rec.arts.marching.misc	Marching-related performance activities.
rec.arts.misc	Arts not covered by other groups.
rec.arts.movies	Movies and movie making.
rec.arts.movies.reviews	Movie reviews. (Moderated)
rec.arts.poems	Postings of poems.
rec.arts.prose	Short fiction and follow-up discussions.
rec.arts.sf.announce	Announcements of science fiction world. (Moderated)
rec.arts.sf.fandom	SF fan activities.
rec.arts.sf.marketplace	SF materials for sale.
rec.arts.sf.misc	Newsgroup for SF lovers.
rec.arts.sf.movies	SF motion pictures.
rec.arts.sf.reviews	Reviews of SF/fantasy/horror works. (Moderated)
rec.arts.sf.science	Real and speculative aspects of SF science.
rec.arts.sf.starwars	Star Wars universe.
rec.arts.sf.tv	Television SF.
rec.arts.sf.written	SF and fantasy prose.
rec.arts.startrek.current	New Star Trek shows, movies, books.
rec.arts.startrek.fandom	Star Trek conventions and memorabilia.
rec.arts.startrek.info	Star Trek universe. (Moderated)
rec.arts.startrek.misc	General discussion of Star Trek.
rec.arts.startrek.reviews	Reviews of Star Trek books, episodes, films, and so on. (Moderated)
rec.arts.startrek.tech	Star Trek's depiction of future technology.
rec.arts.theatre	Stage work and theatre.

Name	Description
rec.arts.tv	The boob tube, its history; discussion of past and current shows.
rec.arts.tv.soaps	Soap operas.
rec.arts.tv.uk	Telly shows from the UK.
rec.arts.wobegon	Discussion of Prairie Home Companion.
rec.audio	High-fidelity audio.
rec.audio.car	Automobile audio systems.
rec.audio.high-end	High-end audio systems. (Moderated)
rec.audio.pro	Professional audio recording and studio engineering.
rec.autos	Automobiles, automotive products, laws.
rec.autos.antique	Automobiles over 25 years old.
rec.autos.driving	Driving automobiles.
rec.autos.marketplace	Buy/sell/trade automobiles, parts, tools, accessories.
rec.autos.misc	Discussion of automobiles.
rec.autos.rod-n-custom	High-performance automobiles.
rec.autos.simulators	Automotive simulators.
rec.autos.sport	Auto competitions.
rec.autos.tech	Technical aspects of automobiles.
rec.autos.vw	Volkswagen products.
rec.aviation.announce	Events for the aviation community. (Moderated)
rec.aviation.answers	Frequently asked questions about aviation. (Moderated)
rec.aviation.homebuilt	Selecting, designing, building, and restoring aircraft.
rec.aviation.ifr	Flying under Instrument Flight Rules.
rec.aviation.military	Military aircraft — past, present, future.
rec.aviation.misc	Topics in aviation.
rec.aviation.owning	Owning airplanes.
rec.aviation.piloting	Discussion for aviators.

rec.aviation.products	Reviews and discussion of products useful to pilots.
rec.aviation.simulators	Flight simulation.
rec.aviation.soaring	Sailplanes and hang gliders.
rec.aviation.stories	Flying anecdotes. (Moderated)
rec.aviation.student	Learning to fly.
rec.backcountry	Outdoors activities.
rec.bicycles.marketplace	Buying, selling, and reviewing cycling items.
rec.bicycles.misc	Discussion of bicycling.
rec.bicycles.racing	Bicycle racing techniques, rules, results.
rec.bicycles.rides	Tours; also, training or commuting routes.
rec.bicycles.soc	Societal issues regarding bicycling.
rec.bicycles.tech	Cycling product design, construction, maintenance, and so on.
rec.birds	Bird watching.
rec.boats	Boating.
rec.boats.paddle	Discussion of boats with oars, paddles, and so on.
rec.climbing	Climbing techniques, competition announcements, and so on.
rec.collecting	Collecting.
rec.collecting.cards	Collecting sport and nonsport cards.
rec.collecting.stamps	Philately.
rec.crafts.brewing	Making beers and meads.
rec.crafts.metalworking	Metalworking.
rec.crafts.misc	Discussion of handiwork arts not covered elsewhere.
rec.crafts.quilting	Quilts and other quilted items.
rec.crafts.textiles	Sewing, weaving, knitting, and other fiber arts.
rec.crafts.winemaking	Winemaking.
rec.equestrian	Things equestrian.

Name	Description
rec.folk-dancing	Folk dances, dancers, and dancing.
rec.food.cooking	Food, cooking, cookbooks, and recipes.
rec.food.drink	Wines and spirits.
rec.food.historic	History of making food.
rec.food.recipes	Recipes. (Moderated)
rec.food.restaurants	Dining out.
rec.food.sourdough	Sourdough.
rec.food.veg	Vegetarians.
rec.gambling	Articles about games of chance and betting.
rec.games.abstract	Perfect information, pure strategy games.
rec.games.backgammon	Backgammon.
rec.games.board	Discussion of and hints about board games.
rec.games.board.ce	Cosmic Encounter (board game).
rec.games.bolo	Bolo (networked strategy war game).
rec.games.bridge	Bridge.
rec.games.chess	Chess, computer chess.
rec.games.chinese-chess	Xiangqi (Chinese chess).
rec.games.corewar	Core War computer challenge.
rec.games.design	Issues related to game design.
rec.games.diplomacy	Diplomacy (conquest game).
rec.games.empire	Empire.
rec.games.frp.advocacy	Flames and rebuttals regarding various role-playing systems.
rec.games.frp.announce	Announcements of role-playing world. (Moderated)
rec.games.frp.archives	Archivable fantasy stories and other projects. (Moderated)
rec.games.frp.cyber	Cyberpunk-related role-playing games.
rec.games.frp.dnd	Fantasy role-playing with TSR's Dungeons & Dragons.

rec.games.frp.live-action	Live-action role-playing games.
rec.games.frp.marketplace	Role-playing game materials — wanted and for sale.
rec.games.frp.misc	Discussion of role-playing games.
rec.games.go	Go.
rec.games.hack	Hack.
rec.games.int-fiction	Discussion of interactive fiction games.
rec.games.mecha	Giant robot games.
rec.games.miniatures	Tabletop wargaming.
rec.games.misc	Games and computer games.
rec.games.moria	Moria.
rec.games.mud.admin	Administrative issues of multiuser dungeons.
rec.games.mud.announce	Articles about multiuser dungeons. (Moderated)
rec.games.mud.diku	DikuMuds.
rec.games.mud.lp	LPMUD (computer role-playing game).
rec.games.mud.misc	Other aspects of multiuser computer games.
rec.games.mud.tiny	Tiny muds (such as MUSH, MUSE, and MOO).
rec.games.netrek	Netrek (XtrekII) (X Window game).
rec.games.pbm	Play-by-mail games.
rec.games.pinball	Pinball-related issues.
rec.games.programmer	Adventure game programming.
rec.games.rogue	Rogue.
rec.games.roguelike.angband	Angband (computer game).
rec.games.roguelike.announce	Information regarding Rogue-style games. (Moderated)
rec.games.roguelike.misc	Rogue-style dungeon games without other groups.
rec.games.trivia	Discussion of trivia.
rec.games.video.3do	3DO video game systems.
rec.games.video.advocacy	Debate over merits of various video game systems.

Name	Description
rec.games.video.arcade	Coin-operated video games.
rec.games.video.arcade.collecting	Collecting, converting, repairing, and so on.
rec.games.video.atari	Atari video game systems.
rec.games.video.classic	Older home video entertainment systems.
rec.games.video.marketplace	Trading or selling home video game stuff.
rec.games.video.misc	Discussion of home video games.
rec.games.video.nintendo	Nintendo video game systems and software.
rec.games.video.sega	Sega video game systems and software.
rec.games.xtank.play	Xtank — strategy and tactics.
rec.games.xtank.programmer	Coding the Xtank game and its robots.
rec.gardens	Gardening — methods and results.
rec.guns	Firearms. (Moderated)
rec.heraldry	Coats of arms.
rec.humor	Jokes and the like. May be offensive.
rec.humor.d	Discussion of rec.humor.
rec.humor.funny	Funny jokes (in the moderator's eyes). (Moderated)
rec.humor.oracle	Advice from the USENET Oracle. (Moderated)
rec.humor.oracle.d	Comments regarding the USENET Oracle's comments.
rec.hunting	Hunting. (Moderated)
rec.juggling	Juggling techniques, equipment, events.
rec.kites	Kites and kiting.
rec.mag	Magazine summaries, tables of contents, and so on.
rec.martial-arts	Martial arts.
rec.misc	Topics regarding recreation/participant sports.

rec.models.railroad	Model railroads.
rec.models.rc	Radio-controlled models.
rec.models.rockets	Model rockets.
rec.models.scale	Model construction.
rec.motorcycles	Motorcycles and related products and laws.
rec.motorcycles.dirt	Riding motorcycles and ATVs off-road.
rec.motorcycles.harley	Harley-Davidson motorcycles.
rec.motorcycles.racing	Racing motorcycles.
rec.music.a-cappella	A capella music.
rec.music.afro-latin	Music with African and Latin influences.
rec.music.beatles	Postings about the Fab Four and their music.
rec.music.bluenote	Jazz, blues, and related music.
rec.music.cd	CDs — availability and other discussions.
rec.music.celtic	Traditional and modern music with a Celtic flavor.
rec.music.christian	Christian music — contemporary and traditional.
rec.music.classical	Classical music.
rec.music.classical.guitar	Classical music performed on guitar.
rec.music.classical.performing	Performing classical (including early) music.
rec.music.compose	Composing music.
rec.music.country.western	Country and western music — performers, performances, and so on.
rec.music.dementia	Comedy and novelty music.
rec.music.dylan	Bob Dylan's works and music.
rec.music.early	Preclassical European music.
rec.music.folk	Folk music.
rec.music.funky	Funk, rap, hip-hop, house, soul, rhythm and blues, and so on.
rec.music.gaffa	Kate Bush and other alternative music. (Moderated)

Name	Description
rec.music.gdead	For (Grateful) Deadheads.
rec.music.indian.classical	Hindustani and Carnatic Indian classical music.
rec.music.indian.misc	Discussion of Indian music.
rec.music.industrial	Industrial-related music styles.
rec.music.info	Music news and announcements. (Moderated)
rec.music.makers	For performers.
rec.music.makers.bass	Upright bass and bass guitar techniques and equipment.
rec.music.makers.guitar	Electric and acoustic guitar techniques and equipment.
rec.music.makers.guitar.acoustic	Acoustic guitar playing.
rec.music.makers.guitar.tablature	Guitar tablature/chords.
rec.music.makers.marketplace	Buying and selling used musical equipment.
rec.music.makers.percussion	Percussion techniques and equipment.
rec.music.makers.synth	Synthesizers and computer music.
rec.music.marketplace	Records, tapes, and CDs: wanted, for sale, and so on.
rec.music.misc	For music lovers.
rec.music.newage	New Age music.
rec.music.phish	Phish.
rec.music.reggae	Roots, rockers, dancehall reggae.
rec.music.reviews	Music reviews. (Moderated)
rec.music.video	Music videos and music video software.
rec.nude	Naturists/nudists.
rec.org.mensa	Talking with Mensa members.
rec.org.sca	Society for Creative Anachronism.
rec.outdoors.fishing	Sport and commercial fishing.
rec.parks.theme	Entertainment theme parks.
rec.pets	Pets, pet care; discussion of household animals.

rec.pets.birds	Culture and care of indoor birds.
rec.pets.cats	Domestic cats.
rec.pets.dogs	Dogs as pets.
rec.pets.herp	Reptiles, amphibians, and other exotic vivarium pets.
rec.photo	Photography.
rec.puzzles	Puzzles, problems, quizzes.
rec.puzzles.crosswords	Making and doing crosswords.
rec.pyrotechnics	Fireworks, rocketry, safety, and other topics.
rec.radio.amateur.antenna	Antennas — theory, techniques, construction.
rec.radio.amateur.digital.misc	Packet radio and other digital radio modes.
rec.radio.amateur.equipment	Production amateur radio hardware.
rec.radio.amateur.homebrew	Amateur radio construction and experimentation.
rec.radio.amateur.misc	Amateur radio practices, contests, events, rules, and so on.
rec.radio.amateur.policy	Radio use and regulation policy.
rec.radio.amateur.space	Amateur radio transmissions through space.
rec.radio.broadcasting	Global domestic broadcast radio. (Moderated)
rec.radio.cb	Citizen-band radio.
rec.radio.info	Postings related to radio. (Moderated)
rec.radio.noncomm	Noncommercial radio.
rec.radio.scanner	"Utility" broadcasting traffic above 30 MHz.
rec.radio.shortwave	Shortwave radio.
rec.radio.swap	Trading and swapping radio equipment.
rec.railroad	For fans of real trains.
rec.roller-coaster	Roller coasters and other amusement park rides.
rec.running	Running for enjoyment, sport, exercise, and so on.
rec.scouting	Worldwide scouting youth organizations.

Name	Description
rec.scuba	SCUBA.
rec.skate	Ice and roller skating.
rec.skiing	Snow skiing.
rec.skydiving	Skydiving.
rec.sport.baseball	Baseball.
rec.sport.baseball.college	Collegiate baseball.
rec.sport.baseball.fantasy	Rotisserie (fantasy) baseball.
rec.sport.basketball.college	Collegiate basketball.
rec.sport.basketball.misc	Basketball.
rec.sport.basketball.pro	Professional basketball.
rec.sport.cricket	Cricket.
rec.sport.cricket.scores	Cricket scores. (Moderated)
rec.sport.disc	Flying disc-based sports.
rec.sport.fencing	Swordplay.
rec.sport.football.australian	Australian (Rules) Football.
rec.sport.football.canadian	Canadian football.
rec.sport.football.college	Collegiate football.
rec.sport.football.fantasy	Rotisserie (fantasy) football.
rec.sport.football.misc	Football.
rec.sport.football.pro	Professional football.
rec.sport.golf	Golfing.
rec.sport.hockey	Ice hockey.
rec.sport.hockey.field	Field hockey.
rec.sport.misc	Spectator sports.
rec.sport.olympics	Olympics.
rec.sport.paintball	Paintball (survival game).
rec.sport.pro-wrestling	Professional wrestling.
rec.sport.rowing	Crew for competition or fitness.
rec.sport.rugby	Rugby.
rec.sport.soccer	Soccer (Association Football).
rec.sport.swimming	Swimming — training and competing.
rec.sport.table-tennis	Table tennis (a.k.a. Ping-Pong).
rec.sport.tennis	Tennis.
rec.sport.triathlon	Multievent sports.
rec.sport.volleyball	Volleyball.
rec.sport.waterski	Waterskiing and other boat-towed activities.

rec.toys.lego	Lego and Duplo (and compatible) toys.
rec.toys.misc	Toys not covered in other groups.
rec.travel	Traveling.
rec.travel.air	Airline travel.
rec.travel.marketplace	Tickets and accommodations — wanted and for sale.
rec.video	Video and video components.
rec.video.cable-tv	Technical and regulatory issues of cable television.
rec.video.production	Making professional-quality video productions.
rec.video.releases	Prerecorded video releases on laserdisc and videotape.
rec.video.satellite	Watching shows via satellite.
rec.windsurfing	Windsurfing.
rec.woodworking	Woodworking.

Sci Groups

Name	*Description*
sci.aeronautics	Aeronautics and related technology. (Moderated)
sci.aeronautics.airliners	Airliner technology. (Moderated)
sci.agriculture	Farming, agriculture, and related topics.
sci.answers	Repository for Usenet articles. (Moderated)
sci.anthropology	Anthropology.
sci.anthropology.paleo	Evolution of man and other primates.
sci.aquaria	Scientific postings about aquaria.
sci.archaeology	Archaeology.
sci.astro	Astronomy.
sci.astro.fits	Issues related to the Flexible Image Transport System.

Name	Description
sci.astro.hubble	Processing Hubble Space Telescope data. (Moderated)
sci.astro.planetarium	Planetariums.
sci.bio	Biology and related sciences.
sci.bio.ecology	Ecology.
sci.bio.ethology	Animal behavior and behavioral ecology.
sci.bio.evolution	Evolutionary biology. (Moderated)
sci.bio.herp	Biology of amphibians and reptiles.
sci.chem	Chemistry and related sciences.
sci.chem.organomet	Organometallic chemistry.
sci.classics	Classical history, languages, art, and more.
sci.cognitive	Perception, memory, judgment, and reasoning.
sci.comp-aided	Computers as tools in scientific research.
sci.cryonics	Suspended animation — theory and practice.
sci.crypt	Methods of data en/decryption.
sci.data.formats	Modeling, storage, and retrieval of scientific data.
sci.econ	Economics.
sci.econ.research	Research in economics. (Moderated)
sci.edu	Education.
sci.electronics	Circuits, electrons, theory, and discussions.
sci.energy	Energy science and technology.
sci.energy.hydrogen	Hydrogen as an alternative fuel.
sci.engr	Technical discussion of engineering tasks.
sci.engr.advanced-tv	HDTV/DATV standards, formats, equipment, practices.
sci.engr.biomed	Biomedical engineering.
sci.engr.chem	Chemical engineering.
sci.engr.civil	Civil engineering.
sci.engr.control	Engineering of control systems.

sci.engr.lighting	Light, vision, and color in architecture, media, and so on.
sci.engr.manufacturing	Manufacturing technology.
sci.engr.mech	Mechanical engineering.
sci.environment	Environment and ecology.
sci.fractals	Objects of nonintegral dimension and other chaos.
sci.geo.fluids	Geophysical fluid dynamics.
sci.geo.geology	Solid earth sciences.
sci.geo.meteorology	Meteorology and related topics.
sci.image.processing	Scientific image processing and analysis.
sci.lang	Natural languages, communication, and so on.
sci.lang.japan	Japanese, oral and written.
sci.life-extension	Slowing, stopping, or reversing the aging process.
sci.logic	Logic — mathematical, philosophical, and computational aspects.
sci.materials	Materials engineering.
sci.math	Mathematical discussions and pursuits.
sci.math.research	Current mathematical research. (Moderated)
sci.math.symbolic	Symbolic algebra.
sci.med	Medicine and related products and regulations.
sci.med.aids	AIDS — treatment, pathology/biology of HIV, prevention. (Moderated)
sci.med.dentistry	Dentistry; teeth.
sci.med.nursing	Nursing.
sci.med.nutrition	Nutrition.
sci.med.occupational	Preventing, detecting, and treating occupational injuries.
sci.med.pharmacy	Pharmaceutical teaching and practice.
sci.med.physics	Physics in medical testing/care.
sci.med.psychobiology	Psychiatry and psychobiology.
sci.med.telemedicine	Clinical consulting through computer networks.

Name	Description
sci.military	Science and the military. (Moderated)
sci.misc	Scientific topics.
sci.nanotech	Self-reproducing molecular-scale machines. (Moderated)
sci.nonlinear	Chaotic systems and other nonlinear scientific study.
sci.op-research	Research, teaching, and application of operations research.
sci.optics	Discussion of optics.
sci.philosophy.tech	Technical philosophy — math, science, logic, and so on.
sci.physics	Physical laws, properties, and so on.
sci.physics.accelerators	Particle accelerators and the physics of beams.
sci.physics.fusion	Fusion (especially cold fusion).
sci.physics.particle	Particle physics.
sci.physics.research	Current physics research. (Moderated)
sci.polymers	Polymer science.
sci.psychology	Psychology.
sci.psychology.digest	PSYCOLOQUY: Refereed Psychology Journal and Newsletter. (Moderated)
sci.research	Research methods, funding, ethics, and so on.
sci.research.careers	Issues related to careers in scientific research.
sci.skeptic	Pseudoscience.
sci.space	Space, space programs, space-related research, and so on.
sci.space.news	Announcements of space-related news. (Moderated)
sci.space.policy	Space policy.
sci.space.science	Space and planetary science and related technical work. (Moderated)
sci.space.shuttle	Space shuttle and the STS program.

sci.space.tech	Issues related to space flight. (Moderated)
sci.stat.consult	Statistical consulting.
sci.stat.edu	Statistics education.
sci.stat.math	Statistics, mathematical.
sci.systems	Systems science.
sci.techniques.microscopy	Microscopy.
sci.techniques.xtallography	Crystallography.
sci.virtual-worlds	Virtual reality — technology and culture. (Moderated)
sci.virtual-worlds.apps	Current and future uses of virtual-worlds technology. (Moderated)

Soc Groups

Name	*Description*
soc.answers	Repository for USENET articles. (Moderated)
soc.bi	Discussion of bisexuality.
soc.college	College, college activities, campus life, and so on.
soc.college.grad	Issues related to graduate schools.
soc.college.gradinfo	Information about graduate schools.
soc.college.org.aiesec	The International Association of Business and Commerce Students.
soc.college.teaching-asst	Issues affecting collegiate teaching assistants.
soc.couples	Discussions for couples (see soc.singles).
soc.couples.intercultural	Intercultural and interracial relationships.
soc.culture.afghanistan	Afghan society.
soc.culture.african	Africa and things African.
soc.culture.african.american	African-American issues.

Name	Description
soc.culture.arabic	Technological and cultural issues, *not* politics.
soc.culture.argentina	Argentina.
soc.culture.asean	Association of Southeast Asian Nations.
soc.culture.asian.american	Issues related to Asian-Americans.
soc.culture.australian	Australia.
soc.culture.austria	Austria.
soc.culture.baltics	Baltic states.
soc.culture.bangladesh	Bangladesh.
soc.culture.bosna-herzgvna	Bosnia-Herzegovina.
soc.culture.brazil	Brazil.
soc.culture.british	Britain and the British.
soc.culture.bulgaria	Bulgaria.
soc.culture.burma	Burma.
soc.culture.canada	Canada.
soc.culture.caribbean	Caribbean.
soc.culture.celtic	Irish, Scottish, Breton, Cornish, Manx, and Welsh.
soc.culture.chile	Chile.
soc.culture.china	China and Chinese culture.
soc.culture.croatia	Croatia.
soc.culture.czecho-slovak	Bohemian, Slovak, Moravian, and Silesian life.
soc.culture.europe	European society.
soc.culture.filipino	Filipino culture.
soc.culture.french	French culture, history, and related topics.
soc.culture.german	German culture and history.
soc.culture.greek	Greece.
soc.culture.hongkong	Hong Kong.
soc.culture.indian	India and things Indian.
soc.culture.indian.info	Information group for soc.culture.indian and so on. (Moderated)
soc.culture.indian.telugu	Telugu.
soc.culture.indonesia	Indonesia.
soc.culture.iranian	Iran and things Iranian/Persian.

soc.culture.israel	Israel and Israelis.
soc.culture.italian	Italians and their culture.
soc.culture.japan	Everything Japanese except the language.
soc.culture.jewish	Jewish culture and religion. (See talk.politics.mideast.)
soc.culture.korean	Korea and things Korean.
soc.culture.laos	Laos.
soc.culture.latin-america	Latin America.
soc.culture.lebanon	Lebanon.
soc.culture.maghreb	North African society and culture.
soc.culture.magyar	Hungarians and their culture.
soc.culture.malaysia	Malaysia.
soc.culture.mexican	Mexico.
soc.culture.misc	Discussion of other cultures.
soc.culture.native	Aboriginal people around the world.
soc.culture.nepal	Nepal.
soc.culture.netherlands	The Netherlands and Belgium.
soc.culture.new-zealand	New Zealand.
soc.culture.nordic	Culture up north.
soc.culture.pakistan	Pakistan.
soc.culture.palestine	Palestine.
soc.culture.peru	Peru.
soc.culture.polish	Poland.
soc.culture.portuguese	Portugal.
soc.culture.romanian	Romanian and Moldavian people.
soc.culture.scientists	Cultural issues regarding scientists and scientific projects.
soc.culture.singapore	Singapore.
soc.culture.soviet	Russian or Soviet culture.
soc.culture.spain	Spain.
soc.culture.sri-lanka	Sri Lanka.
soc.culture.taiwan	Taiwan.
soc.culture.tamil	Tamil language, history, and culture.
soc.culture.thai	Thailand.
soc.culture.turkish	Turkey.

`soc.culture.ukrainian`	Ukraine.
`soc.culture.uruguay`	Uruguay.
`soc.culture.usa`	United States of America.
`soc.culture.venezuela`	Venezuela.
`soc.culture.vietnamese`	Vietnamese culture.
`soc.culture.yugoslavia`	Yugoslavia.
`soc.feminism`	Feminism and feminist issues. (Moderated)
`soc.history`	Things historical.
`soc.libraries.talk`	Libraries.
`soc.men`	Issues related to men, their problems, and relationships.
`soc.misc`	Socially oriented topics not in other groups.
`soc.motss`	Homosexuality.
`soc.net-people`	Announcements, requests, and so on about people on the Net.
`soc.penpals`	In search of Net.friendships.
`soc.politics`	Political problems, systems, solutions. (Moderated)
`soc.politics.arms-d`	Arms discussion digest. (Moderated)
`soc.religion.bahai`	Baha'i Faith. (Moderated)
`soc.religion.christian`	Christianity and related topics. (Moderated)
`soc.religion.christian.bible-study`	Examining the Holy Bible. (Moderated)
`soc.religion.eastern`	Eastern religions. (Moderated)
`soc.religion.islam`	Islam. (Moderated)
`soc.religion.quaker`	Religious Society of Friends.
`soc.religion.shamanism`	The shamanic experience. (Moderated)
`soc.rights.human`	Human rights and activism (for example, Amnesty International).
`soc.roots`	Genealogy and genealogical matters.
`soc.singles`	Newsgroup for single people, their activities, and so on.
`soc.veterans`	Social issues related to military veterans.
`soc.women`	Issues related to women, their problems, and relationships.

Talk Groups

Name	Description
talk.abortion	Discussion of and arguments regarding abortion.
talk.answers	Repository for USENET articles. (Moderated)
talk.bizarre	The unusual, bizarre, curious, and often stupid.
talk.environment	The state of the environment and what to do.
talk.origins	Evolution vs. creationism (sometimes hot!).
talk.philosophy.misc	Philosophical musings.
talk.politics.animals	Animal use and/or abuse.
talk.politics.china	Political issues related to China.
talk.politics.crypto	Cryptography and government.
talk.politics.drugs	Politics of drug issues.
talk.politics.guns	Politics of firearm ownership and (mis)use.
talk.politics.medicine	Politics and ethics regarding health care.
talk.politics.mideast	Discussion of and debate over the Middle East.
talk.politics.misc	Political discussions and ravings.
talk.politics.soviet	Soviet politics, domestic and foreign.
talk.politics.space	Nontechnical issues affecting space exploration.
talk.politics.theory	Theory of politics and political systems.
talk.politics.tibet	Tibet.
talk.rape	Discussion on stopping rape; not to be crossposted.
talk.religion.misc	Religious, ethical, and moral implications.
talk.religion.newage	Esoteric and minority religions and philosophies.
talk.rumors	Postings of rumors.

K12 Groups

K12Net is a collection of conferences devoted to K-12 educational curricula, language exchanges with native speakers, and classroom-to-classroom projects designed by teachers. The groups are distributed via FidoNet and Usenet.

Classroom-to-classroom projects comprise the `k12.sys` hierarchy; they are featured in K12 *Channels*, which are periodically reassigned based on usage and appropriate project length.

Forums for casual conversation among students are divided by grade level in the `k12.chat` hierarchy; teachers also can exchange general ideas about using telecommunications in education.

For more information, contact a member of the K12Net Council of Coordinators:

Jack Crawford (`jack@rochgate.fidonet.org`)

Janet Murray (`jmurray@psg.com`)

Rob Reilly (`rreilly@athena.mit.edu`)

Mort Sternheim (`sternheim@phast.umass.edu`)

Louis Van Geel (`lvg@psg.com`)

Name	Description
`k12.ed.art`	Arts and crafts curricula in K-12.
`k12.ed.business`	Business curricula in K-12.
`k12.ed.comp.literacy`	Teaching computer literacy in K-12.
`k12.ed.health-pe`	Health and physical education curricula in K-12.
`k12.ed.life-skills`	Home economics, career education, and school counseling.
`k12.ed.math`	Mathematics curricula in K-12.
`k12.ed.music`	Music and performing arts curricula in K-12.
`k12.ed.science`	Science curricula in K-12.
`k12.ed.soc-studies`	Social studies and history curricula in K-12.
`k12.ed.special`	Educating students with disabilities and/or special needs.

k12.ed.tag	Educating gifted and talented students.
k12.ed.tech	Industrial arts and vocational education in K-12.
k12.library	Implementing information technologies in school libraries.
k12.lang.art	Teaching language skills in K-12.
k12.lang.deutsch-eng	Bilingual German/English practice with native speakers.
k12.lang.esp-eng	Bilingual Spanish/English practice with native speakers.
k12.lang.francais	French practice with native speakers.
k12.lang.russian	Bilingual Russian/English practice with native speakers.
k12.sys.projects	Discussion of potential projects.
k12.sys.channel0	Current projects.
k12.sys.channel1	Current projects.
k12.sys.channel2	Current projects.
k12.sys.channel3	Current projects.
k12.sys.channel4	Current projects.
k12.sys.channel5	Current projects.
k12.sys.channel6	Current projects.
k12.sys.channel7	Current projects.
k12.sys.channel8	Current projects.
k12.sys.channel9	Current projects.
k12.sys.channel10	Current projects.
k12.sys.channel11	Current projects.
k12.sys.channel12	Current projects.
k12.chat.elementary	Casual conversation for students in grades K-5.
k12.chat.junior	Casual conversation for students in grades 6-8.
k12.chat.senior	Casual conversation for high school students.
k12.chat.teacher	Casual conversation for K-12 teachers.

Alt Groups

Alt groups are not subject to the formal process used to create groups of other types. As a result, some alt groups appear and disappear on a daily basis. Some are notably uncensored.

For a partial listing of groups in the alt hierarchy, see *The Internet For Dummies*, Chapter 12, section "More Hierarchies."

This list of newsgroups is adapted from one originally written by Gene Spafford, now at Purdue University, and currently edited by David C. Lawrence of UUNET Technologies, and is reproduced with their permission.

The list of newsgroup changes nearly every week, and most Usenet sites carry only a selection of the avaliable groups, so what's available on your site will not be exactly what's listed here.

Index

Symbols

A

B

C

D

E

G

H

I

J

K

L

M

P

Q

R

S

X

Z

Notes

Notes

Notes

IDG BOOKS WORLDWIDE REGISTRATION CARD

RETURN THIS REGISTRATION CARD FOR FREE CATALOG

Title of this book: THE INTERNET FOR DUMMIES QR

My overall rating of this book: ❑ Very good [1] ❑ Good [2] ❑ Satisfactory [3] ❑ Fair [4] ❑ Poor [5]

How I first heard about this book:

❑ Found in bookstore; name: [6] ❑ Book review: [7]

❑ Advertisement: [8] ❑ Catalog: [9]

❑ Word of mouth; heard about book from friend, co-worker, etc.: [10] ❑ Other: [11]

What I liked most about this book:

What I would change, add, delete, etc., in future editions of this book:

Other comments:

Number of computer books I purchase in a year: ❑ 1 [12] ❑ 2-5 [13] ❑ 6-10 [14] ❑ More than 10 [15]

I would characterize my computer skills as: ❑ Beginner [16] ❑ Intermediate [17] ❑ Advanced [18] ❑ Professional [19]

I use ❑ DOS [20] ❑ Windows [21] ❑ OS/2 [22] ❑ Unix [23] ❑ Macintosh [24] ❑ Other: [25] ____________ (please specify)

I would be interested in new books on the following subjects:
(please check all that apply, and use the spaces provided to identify specific software)

❑ Word processing: [26] ❑ Spreadsheets: [27]

❑ Data bases: [28] ❑ Desktop publishing: [29]

❑ File Utilities: [30] ❑ Money management: [31]

❑ Networking: [32] ❑ Programming languages: [33]

❑ Other: [34]

I use a PC at (please check all that apply): ❑ home [35] ❑ work [36] ❑ school [37] ❑ other: [38] ____________

The disks I prefer to use are ❑ 5.25 [39] ❑ 3.5 [40] ❑ other: [41] ____________

I have a CD ROM: ❑ yes [42] ❑ no [43]

I plan to buy or upgrade computer hardware this year: ❑ yes [44] ❑ no [45]

I plan to buy or upgrade computer software this year: ❑ yes [46] ❑ no [47]

Name: Business title: [48]

Type of Business: [49]

Address (❑ home [50] ❑ work [51]/Company name:)

Street/Suite#

City [52]/State [53]/Zipcode [54]: Country [55]

❑ **I liked this book!**
You may quote me by name in future IDG Books Worldwide promotional materials.

My daytime phone number is ____________

IDG BOOKS

THE WORLD OF COMPUTER KNOWLEDGE

☐ **YES!**

Please keep me informed about IDG's World of Computer Knowledge. Send me the latest IDG Books catalog.

NO POSTAGE
NECESSARY
IF MAILED
IN THE
UNITED STATES

BUSINESS REPLY MAIL

FIRST CLASS MAIL PERMIT NO. 2605 SAN MATEO, CALIFORNIA

IDG Books Worldwide
155 Bovet Rd
San Mateo CA 94402-9833